Fashion Designers' Sketchbooks

Fashion Designers'

Sketchbooks

Hywel Davies

Laurence King Publishing

Fashion Designers' Sketchbooks # INTRODUCTION

explores the creative processes of
contemporary fashion practitioners. For designers,
sketchbooks are companions that capture and facilitate
research, support design development and communicate
new fashion ideas. Going beyond an instrument for
drawing, sketchbooks secure a varied range of material
that inspires, fuels and transforms initial fashion ideas
into final concepts.

The creative process for fashion designers does not pursue a set routine or course. Designers
have their own methods and idiosyncrasies that determine their working process. *Fashion
Designers' Sketchbooks* celebrates how designers transform two-dimensional ideas into
three-dimensional outcomes. From conception to completion, from first inspirations to
catwalk collections, all is captured in these unique, creative and captivating sketchbooks.
'Curiosity is the most important thing' to initiate a design process believes John Galliano.
**'I think you have to be curious and have the courage of your own convictions. I start
with research and from there I build the muse, the idea, tell a story and develop a
character, a look and then a collection.'** As an expert in narration, Galliano is renowned
for his storytelling. His inspirational global research trips produce beautiful research books,
and Galliano believes the creative journey is integral to the essence of his work.
'I always like there to be a bit of a story to each collection,' admits Peter Jensen, who uses
a sketchbook to develop his fictional characters or muse for his collections.
Richard Nicoll endorses the value of research, *'It is very important, it defines and reflects the
themes of the collection'*, while Deryck Walker identifies his perception of research: *'It can
be a word, a picture or twenty pictures, it's whatever opens your head and gets you.'*
Antonio Marras, creative director of Kenzo, believes inspiration can be taken from everything.
**'I need many things to nourish my inspiration: objects, images, stories and pieces of cloth.
I continuously need to see new things, new places, to meet new people to listen to.'**
'My inspiration comes from literally anywhere,' explains Matthew Williamson. *'As a designer,
it is vital to be as open as possible to new ideas. My training at Central Saint Martins taught
me to compile and develop that inspiration into a clear intention from which I could begin
my research.'*
Creative director for Vivienne Westwood, Andreas Kronthaler considers inspiration as a key
part of everyday life. *'I'm a very visual person. The process could involve a piece of literature,
a photograph or pictures; they are all influences, however, I don't go out looking for them.
Inspiration is everywhere and my work is a development, so it goes on, and an idea can be
stretched for seasons as I refine it.'*
'Anything and everything,' also inspires Hamish Morrow. **'Nothing is sacred in the fuelling
of creation. The best part is dreaming up a collection in the beginning and putting it down
on paper. The hardest part is making it real and executing it with perfection.'**

Graeme Black, too, enjoys the beginning of a collection where, *'Everything still seems possible. Every new collection is like a new beginning. That sense of excitement when an idea clicks in your mind is so rewarding.'*

The essence of research according to Aitor Throup is, *'When you don't feel like you're doing research, when you're simply exposing yourself to things that interest you or inspire you in some way.'*

'Creativity cannot be given a timetable,' cautions Antonio Ciutto. **'It comes when it comes, or not for that matter.'** Tim Soar sees the creative process as a cathartic outlet: *'I think many designers design because they are compelled to. That does not mean the process is unpleasant, but it is not necessarily enjoyable in the normal sense of the word. I just do what I have to do to feed my habit. That habit happens to be design.'* Dries Van Noten also sees the constant creative pursuit as a stimulant; *'It is more or less our drug.'*

'It starts from our guts and our minds,' describes New York-based designers Duckie Brown. **'We have a strong feeling of what we are going to do and then proceed. It's the most wonderful, frightening, exciting process in the world. At times it is effortless and at other times it's just hard work.'**

Sketchbooks are vehicles for research, exploration and the resolution of ideas. *Fashion Designers' Sketchbooks* explores how designers design, how they initiate ideas and the journey they then endure to realize their goal. It investigates when designers are most prolific and what materials they assemble to ease their often erratic and creative journey.

'A bad workman blames his tools,' notes Dries Van Noten. *'It is more a question of spirit than materials.'* Other designers choose to employ certain implements, from specific pencils to precise types of paper, to maintain their design process.

Routines and rituals are also part of the process. Working during nocturnal hours is a reoccurring theme. *'I've always felt a sort of creative energy at night,'* states Aitor Throup. *'I love the feeling that I'm the last one up. My thoughts are much clearer and I feel calmer.'* Carola Euler shares this view. **'At night is when everything happens. I didn't know that people were actually creative at any other time of day.'**

Designers regard their design studio as a nucleus of activity, a base and a sanctuary. However, planes, trains and hotel rooms are often a reality for working environments, making the sketchbook the dependable device in which to gather and develop fashion ideas.

As an embryonic platform for thoughts, sketchbooks foster designers' sensibilities and provide an environment where they can select, edit and rework concepts. Nurturing notes, scribbles, collages, photographs, design drawings, toile work, line-ups, fabric swatches and illustrations, sketchbooks are the medium by which designers communicate their inspiration and cultivate fearless new visions.

Sketchbooks provide a personal place for artistic insecurities to be worked out, viewpoints to be resolved and ultimately a space where fashion is brought to life. Celebrating the view that the creative process is as enlightening, dynamic and stimulating as the final garments, *Fashion Designers' Sketchbooks* is a unique glimpse into the minds, lives and creativity of contemporary fashion designers.

How important is research in your working process?

Research is what defines each season or collection. It starts with the very first decision to make the new collection and, from that point on, everything that enters the arena plays a part as research. So, at that stage I try to surround myself with what I understand to be the 'right' stuff for that season, including good books, films and images.

Is there a specific time of day when you are most creative?

Creativity cannot be given a timetable, it comes when it comes, or not for that matter.

How would you describe your design process?

It varies from season to season. It might be fluid, pragmatic, chaotic or organized, but it is never linear. We chase after an unrealized goal.

6 ⅞ (SIX AND SEVEN EIGHTHS)

Antonio Ciutto and David Wojtowycz make up Six and Seven Eighths, a partnership that was established in 2006. Born in South Africa, Ciutto studied architecture before gaining an MA in Fashion Design at Central Saint Martins in London. Ukrainian David Wojtowycz studied Fine Art at Goldsmiths in London, going on to work as a children's book illustrator. 6 ⅞ is not bound by a concept or design philosophy, but focuses on technique, research and pattern cutting to produce dramatic and radical ideas for clothing.

Do you have sources of inspiration that you always revisit?

I always try to gain access to museum archives to view vintage collections. I usually revisit those whom I consider the great fashion masters of all time: Vionnet, Charles James, Balenciaga and Dior. I always come back to them when I am feeling lost. What interests me usually is pattern and construction. I do not take a surface interest, but try to understand from their perspectives.

Is there a routine to your design process?

Design is very different from production or manufacture; it is a very lengthy process for me. Once I spent three weeks working on a shoulder seam that in the end did not work out. Sometimes I enlist the help of other people to give an objective view of my own drawings – sometimes it is hard to see what a drawing actually looks like, means or contains.

What materials are essential to your working methods?

Literally anything that is in my vicinity. I have a tendency to lose stationery even within arm's reach, so I usually have many of each thing spread everywhere in my studio. I use a lot of paper for quick pattern ideas, so I always have scissors, measuring tapes, masking tape, sketchbooks and notebooks. I always need to describe things using quick sketches to seamstresses and workers.

What is the most enjoyable part of designing for you?

Although I love a real physical outcome, it is the process of getting something from nothing that interests me most. Sometimes it is the 'getting lost' that is most interesting.

What fuels your design ideas?

I am never interested in just a visual or surface thing, but rather the process behind the creation of that thing.

A mock-up of a dress from 6 ⅞'s Spring/ Summer 07 collection is made in toile. The prototype garment is made exactly half its intended size so the designers can see if the proportions work appropriately.

Working at half the intended size, sections of garments are made from toile and put on mannequins. From the Spring/Summer 07 collection.

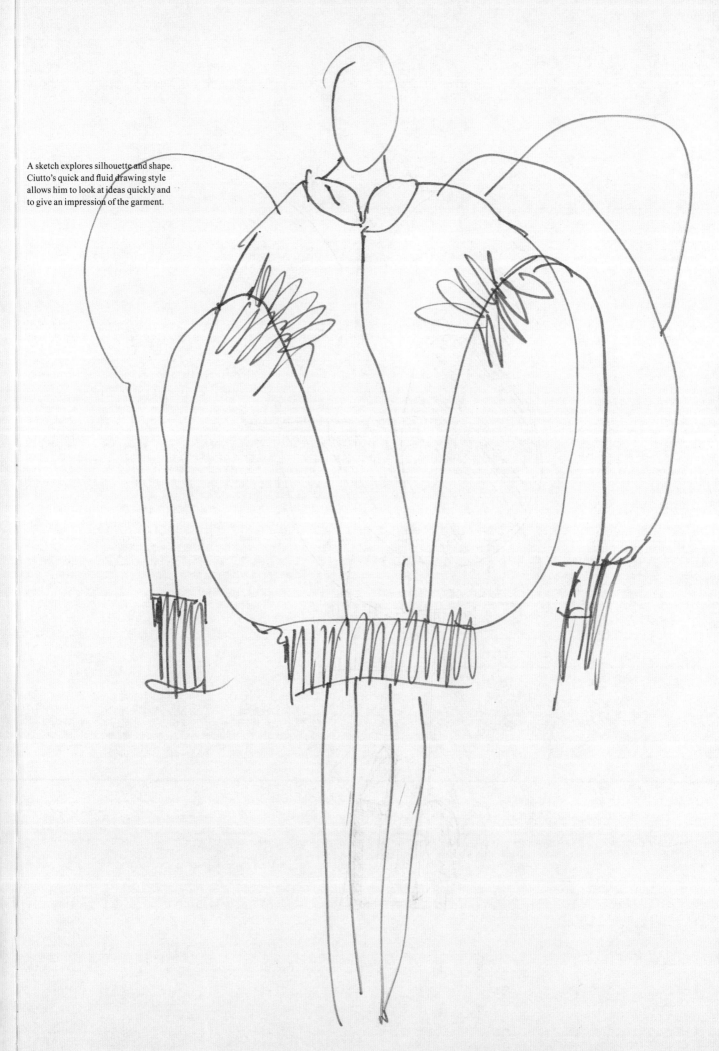

A sketch explores silhouette and shape. Ciutto's quick and fluid drawing style allows him to look at ideas quickly and to give an impression of the garment.

Fabric research book for the Spring/Summer 07 collection. Information recorded in the book includes suppliers' details and the cost of the fabric.

£60 ± p.m
Joel + Son

Joel +
Pongees
silk
organza
£32.90
p.m.

140 wide

H.B. (Paris
£24.9

£60

Viscose
£

anza A
ons.
6 14 49

Tel (44) 020-7739 9330
Fax (44) 020-7739 9332
E-Mail: info@pongees.co.uk
Website: www.pongees.co.uk
...oxton Square
...don N1 6NN
...LIMITED

447W - 1
VISCOSE/SILK SATIN

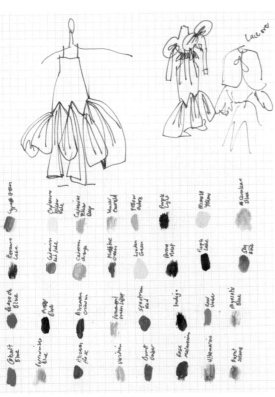

Antonio Ciutto's ongoing sketchbook pages relate to no specific season but show the designer's exploration of garment shape and silhouette. The swatches indicate an investigation of colour for the garments.

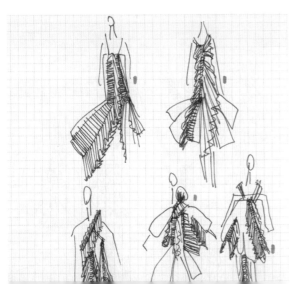

KNITWEAR

INSETS - RIBBON
LACE
PLEATING

Is there a routine to your design process?

The journey can follow a similar pattern, but that is just the way my research is presented; my thoughts are always developing and I push myself to question the process every time.

What is the best environment for you to work in?

My parents' dining room. I don't live there but I am so relaxed there that it brings out some of my best collages. They are two of my greatest friends so it's easy to be in and out of their company while I work and get away from the constant phone calls at the studio!!

What is the most enjoyable part of designing for you?

The moment you know you are on to something is the most exciting. But, I enjoy all aspects of the process. I think sometimes that it's difficult not to be more sociable with work, but then would I be achieving and focusing if there were a lot of people interacting with me all of the time?

What materials are essential to your working methods?

The right-coloured paper to present my research on, some tracing paper and a mechanical pencil.

How does your research and design work evolve from 2D to 3D?

I try to get the 2D as close as I can to the 3D before we start pattern cutting, but I also realize that I am designing and researching at every stage of the process. Sometimes through pattern cutting a great new shape emerges and an entirely new design presents itself to me through 3D exploration.

How important is research in your working process?

Research is constant. I don't necessarily research in order to start a project. It's something that I am constantly doing in one way or another.

AIMEE McWILLIAMS

Defining her modern approach to fashion, Aimee McWilliams debuted her Autumn/ Winter 04/05 collection at London Fashion Week in 2004, just a year after graduating from Central Saint Martins. McWilliams is known for her forward-thinking approach to fashion design, and through creative pattern cutting and the imaginative use of fabric, she creates avant-garde clothing. Successfully balancing work as a designer, illustrator and stylist, McWilliams embraces all aspects of the fashion industry. Her originality was rewarded in 2006 when she was named Scottish Designer of the Year.

How would you describe your design process?

I like to be free to explore new thoughts and to be undefined by a definitive theme, so my process is more of a concept resulting from my unique blend of research. Thought and personal, internal dialogue is a very important part of my process. I take photos, I collect visuals, I write down my internal dialogue and I try out new ways of letting go and exploring and restraining and refining.

What fuels your design ideas?

Obscure films from the late 1960s and early 1970s. I often take stills from the screen to play with.

Is there a specific time of day when you are most creative?

No, I can be creative anytime. I just don't think as clearly when deprived of too much sleep!!

This collage by Aimee McWilliams inspired a showpiece black jersey dress for her Autumn/Winter 06/07 collection and was photographed on Lily Cole for Italian *Vogue*. The vast quantity of draped silk was visually translated from this collage.

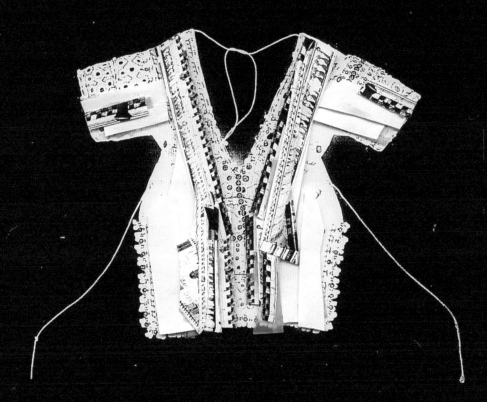

do in negative.
x2

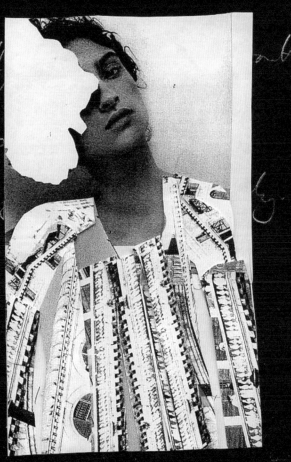

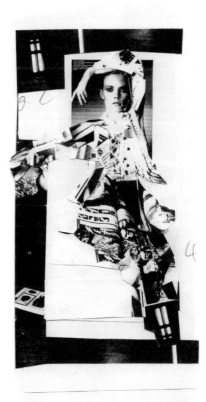

ed in the basement in
:s)

OPPOSITE — For Spring /Summer 07
an artwork illustrates a direct link from a
collage created by Aimee McWilliams to
the real garment. 'I often use collage merely
as a starting point to sketch and design, but
this time the answer was already there.'
TOP LEFT — A collage for Spring/Summer
04 is used by the designer as a continual
reference in later collections.
BOTTOM LEFT — For Autumn/Winter
07/08, McWilliams again used collage to
communicate the spirit of the collection.
She explains, 'I used this image to design
and rework an idea.'
TOP RIGHT — This image inspired the
furs in the Autumn/Winter 07/08 collection.
'I had the furs dyed this beautiful caramel
yellow leaving all the guard hairs black,
as inspired by this image. This page also
inspired the cast bodice work I was
commissioning at the time.'
BOTTOM RIGHT — An inspiration
collage for jacket ideas for the Spring/
Summer 06 collection.

How important is research in your working process?

I think my work itself is the research process. In some ways, my life also becomes the research process. I can't really engage with the traditional 'linear' sense of the research process, where there's a prelude to the design process when information is gathered and edited to inspire a direction. I have recently been attempting to implement a version of that into my own way of working, to add to the existing root or core of the design to further inform it. But, in general, I usually research new solutions to the problems I invent (in terms of design) through storytelling and illustration. The result of the explorative and experimental process is the product, the final design.

What is the most enjoyable part of designing for you?

The enjoyable, and valuable, part of the research process is when you don't feel like you're doing research, when you're simply exposing yourself to things that interest you or inspire you in some way. The process, for me, then becomes about deciphering meaning.

Is there a specific time of day when you are most creative?

Definitely at night. I've always felt a sort of creative energy when I know that it's quiet on the street and that everyone's tucked up in bed; I love the feeling that I'm the last one up. My thoughts are much clearer and I feel calmer.

Born to Argentinean parents in 1980, Aitor Throup graduated from London's Royal College of Art in 2006. He received awards from Umbro, Evisu and Levi's before leaving college and his graduate menswear collection won the Fashion Collection of the Year Award at 'ITS#FIVE' (International Talent Support) Fashion Awards in 2006, establishing Throup as an innovative menswear designer.

AITOR THROUP

How would you describe your design process?

It's an exploration, through drawings, sculptures and garments to find new solutions and to invent new objects. My design process is 50% inventing unique situations that create unique problems and 50% finding equally unique ways to solve those problems. I'm very interested in the idea of rejecting the responsibility of making aesthetic decisions for the final piece. My design process is often about designing the process rather than the product; I love the idea of an incidental outcome that you couldn't possibly imagine without actually going through the process. As long as the process and the story or concept make sense, then something beautiful (or at least interesting) should come out at the other end.

What materials are essential to your working methods?

H, HB and 2B pencils, a good rubber, a portable watercolour case with my watercolour rag to control the water, basic black and red Bic ballpoint pens, good paper/sketchbooks (medium texture, off-white, heavier-than-cartridge-but-lighter-than-watercolour paper), plasticine or plaster, pattern paper and a pattern master, fabrics, masking tape, pins and a sewing machine.

Do you experience a 'eureka moment' when you know a design is working?

As my process is heavily ideas-based rather than trend-based, it has led me to some quite scary situations in the past where I haven't known exactly how some key outfits are going to look until literally the night before a show. A lot of the time, my work is only fully 'designed' once the idea is fully 'resolved', which sometimes means that we're resolving an idea up until the moment we show it to the viewer. So I guess that our 'eureka moment' is more often than not a feeling of relief.

Do you have sources of inspiration that you always revisit?

Definitely. Once I find something that truly inspires me I tend to kind of get obsessed with it and never let go; it seems to remain relevant regardless of time passing. I could never just be inspired by something for three months and go off it after that. I'm loyal to my sources of inspiration. For example, there are two books that have been constant sources of inspiration for me since I started studying 'fashion': *Goad: The Many Moods of Phil Hale* by Phil Hale and *Jimmy Corrigan: The Smartest Kid on Earth* by Chris Ware. They are both unique geniuses who have found incredibly well-defined, personal ways of communicating. I still learn so much from both those books every time I pick them up. I also owe a lot to Leonardo da Vinci, Dieter Rams [German industrial designer], Spring Hurlbut [Canadian artist], Berlinde De Bruyckere [Belgian artist] and others.

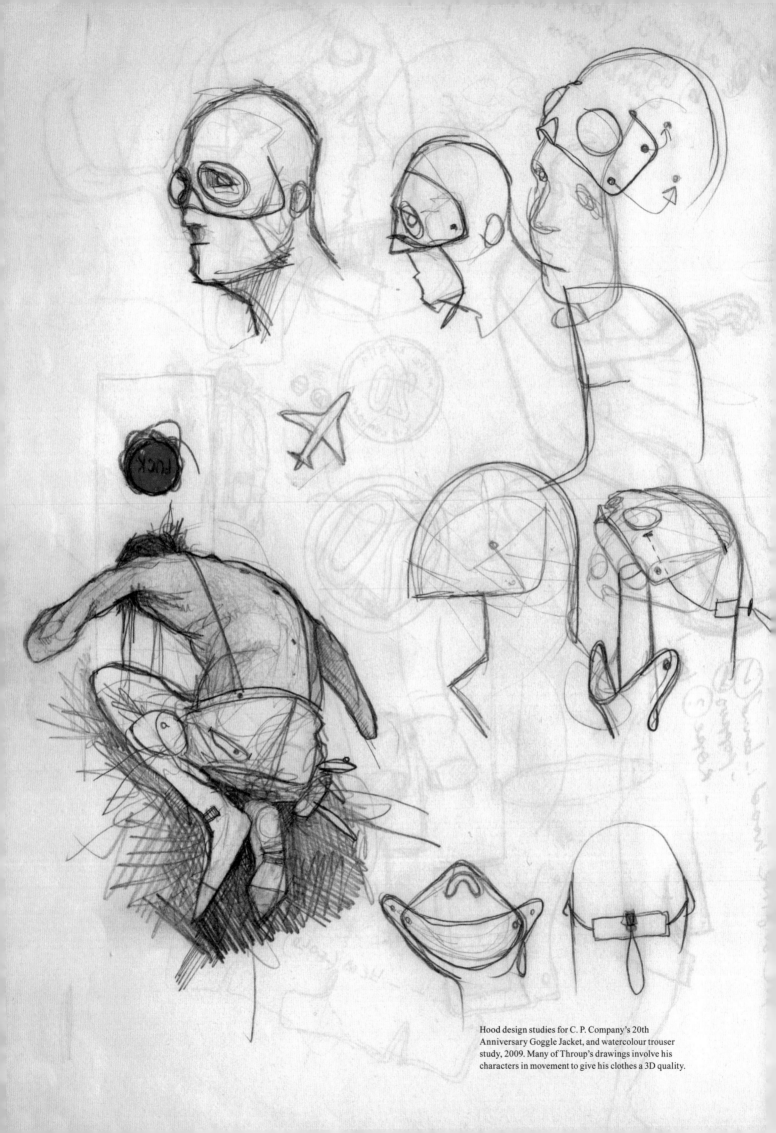

Hood design studies for C. P. Company's 20th
Anniversary Goggle Jacket, and watercolour trouser
study, 2009. Many of Throup's drawings involve his
characters in movement to give his clothes a 3D quality.

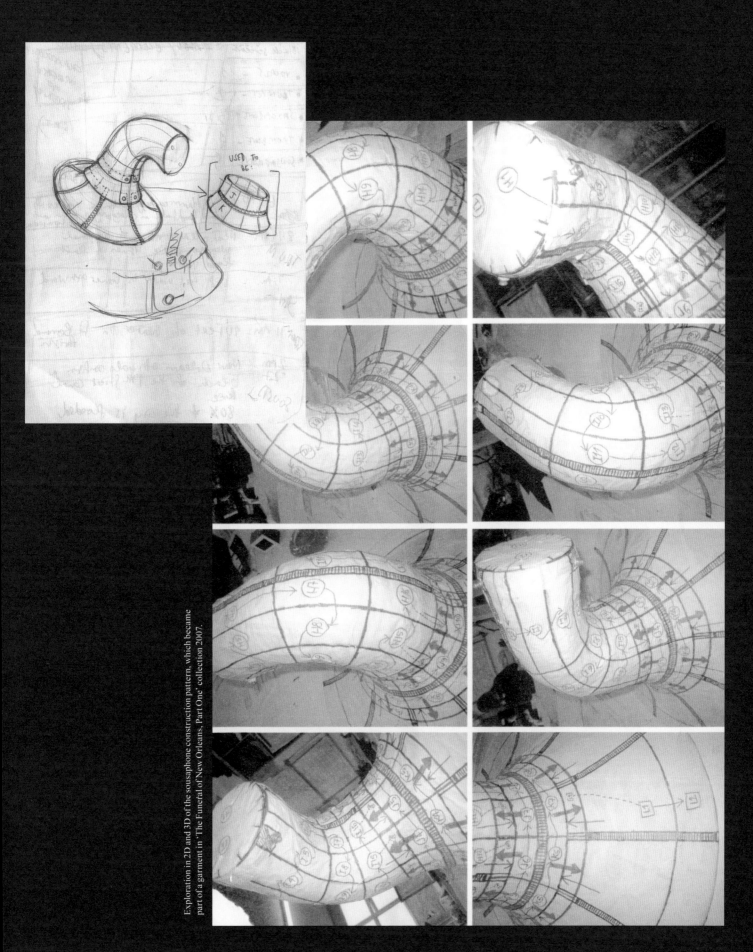

Exploration in 2D and 3D of the sousaphone construction pattern, which became part of a garment in 'The Funeral of New Orleans, Part One' collection 2007.

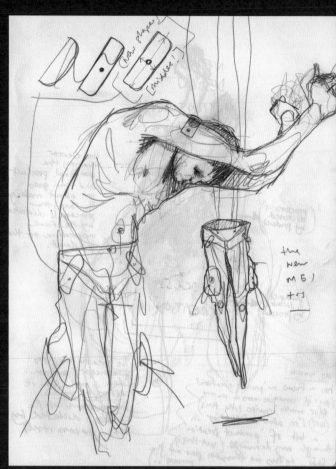

TOP RIGHT — Design study sketches for Stone Island's 'Articulated Anatomy' trousers, March 2008.
BOTTOM RIGHT — A page from Throup's personal sketchbook, showing the designer exploring garments and accessories on moving characters, 2009.

TOP LEFT — Shirt and shoulder drawing exploring details, 2007.
BOTTOM LEFT — A preliminary sketch for Topman's 'Black Trouser Project', June 2008.

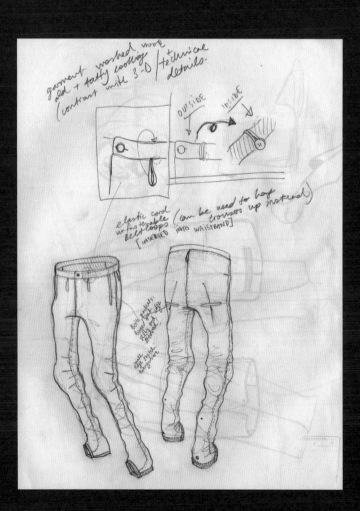

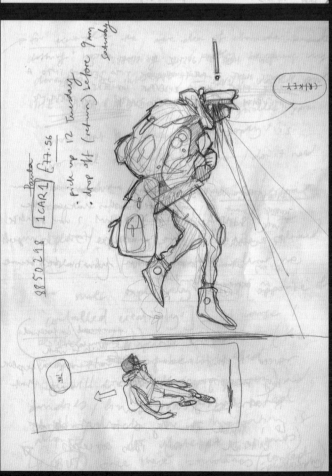

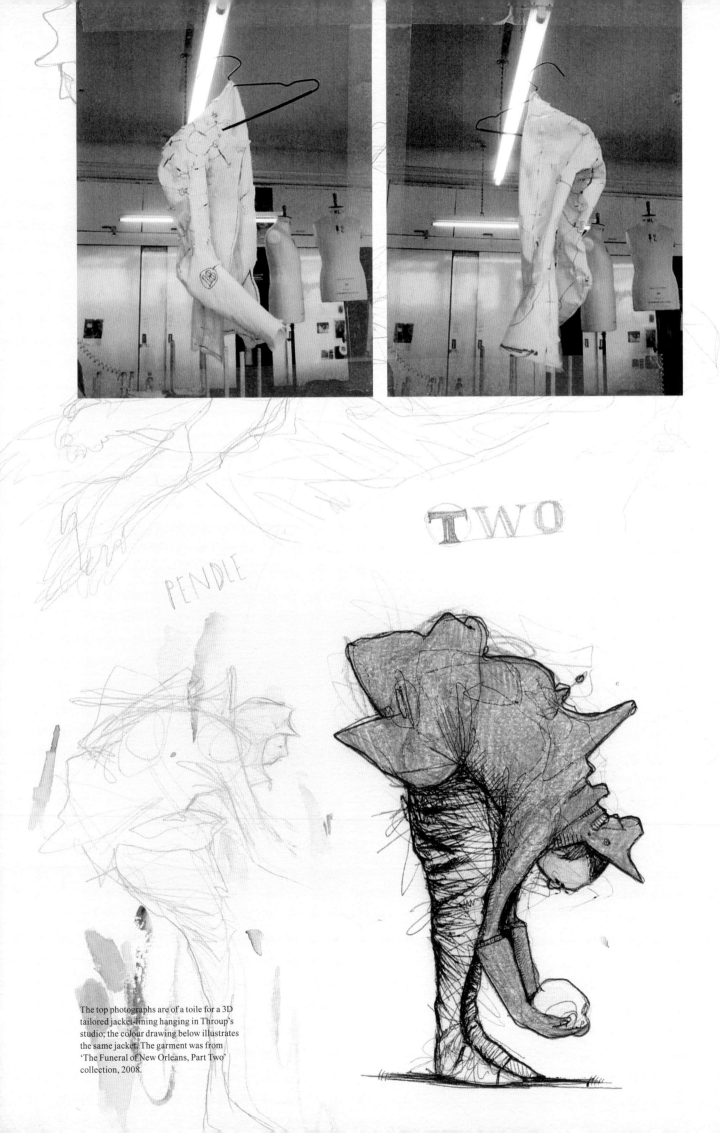

TWO

PENDLE

The top photographs are of a toile for a 3D tailored jacket-lining hanging in Throup's studio; the colour drawing below illustrates the same jacket. The garment was from 'The Funeral of New Orleans, Part Two' collection, 2008.

What is the most enjoyable part of designing for you?

Sourcing, playing and experimenting. Ideas are aplenty and it is the edit that can be the hardest part as options are endless. The most satisfying moment is first seeing the whole collection hanging together.

It involves a huge amount of photography and sketching – I am never without a camera and a sketchbook. Linking seven yearly collections cohesively would be impossible without these tools.

ALICE TEMPERLEY

Alice Temperley trained at London's Central Saint Martins and went on to study a Masters degree in fabric technology and print at the Royal College of Art. Temperley London was launched during London Fashion Week in 2000 and has become synonymous with glamour, craftsmanship and beautiful fabrics. The first Temperley boutique opened in London's Notting Hill in 2002, and three further stand-alone stores have opened their doors in New York, Los Angeles and Dubai. Temperley produces seven collections a year, including Ready-To-Wear, Bridal, Accessories and Black Label (a collection of evening dresses). With fabric being a major focus of her collections, Temperley is renowned for her prints, embroideries and acute attention to detail.

What is the best environment for you to work in?

I have a wonderful studio at the top of one of our distribution warehouses. It is a huge room with vaulted ceilings and surround windows with views over London. This room is the perfect environment for creativity and also where I store my archive, so I can work here without any disruption for hours on end.

How would you describe your design process?
It's personal, organic, fluid and eclectic.

How important is research in your working process?

My research is essential and is something I am always doing no matter where I am or what I am doing. Travel and markets play a large part in this, as inspiration can be found in anything and anywhere. If I like something I believe I will forever and I buy it for its interest, be it the colour, the shape or the proportion. My archive is constantly being added to and is a permanent source of inspiration.

Do you have sources of inspiration that you always revisit?
I always refer to my treasured archive of thousands of swatches and fabrics. I have a true love of pattern, and my design process keeps me engaged permanently, as it has since I was a child.

What materials are essential to your working methods?

I keep it simple: I use refillable lead pencils, fine liners, a calligraphy pen and a few Pantone pens for colour.

Is there a routine to your design process?

I start by gathering story ideas and I build my collection's mood around print, colour, detail and embellishments. Then, I design into each story, working out how the muse would wear the clothes.

TOP — From Deauville to Biarritz, the French seaside scenes of the 1930s inspired the Temperley Spring/Summer 08 collection. Entitled 'Plage Privée', the collection is influenced by historical bathing costumes. **BOTTOM** — A mood board for Temperley London's Autumn /Winter 07/08 collection called 'Beauty in Exile'. The collection draws inspiration from Paris in the early 1900s with the arrival of Russian nobility, artists and their muses. Inspired by these glamorous émigrés, Parisian society was enraptured by the vivid and exotic scenes played out before them by Diaghilev's Ballets Russes. The mood board shows how photography, fabric and historical references are brought together.

Do you have a team that is involved in the design process? If so, what do they do?

I am superstitious and very faithful. I always work with the same people and I like having my team. I love having a steady core I can count on. And I need the energy of young people who come from different places in the world with new and fresh visions – and not only from fashion.

How would you describe your design process?

My creative process is a compromise between new and old. A balance between memories and future, traditions and experiments. I do not make distinctions of any sort; everything goes through my eyes and then something suddenly strikes me – even the smallest thing – and gives me inspiration for the next collection.

How does your research and design work evolve from 2D to 3D?

From thinking up a collection, to drawing it, to creating patterns then prototypes – I like the magical chemistry that makes all these phases work together in the end.

Kenzo Takada was born in Japan in 1939. He studied at Tokyo's Bunka Fashion College before establishing his fashion house, Kenzo, in Paris in 1970. For over 20 years, Takada brought an eclectic range of influences to fashion and was revered for promoting the diversity and compatibility of ethnic styles and cultural elements from all parts of the world. Takada was recognized for his ability to interpret styles and specific costumes from various parts of the world and assimilate them into a radical internationalism.

ANTONIO MARRAS
for
KENZO

Is there a routine to your design process?

My starting point is always the same: an accurate research of materials and fabrics and the way they can be used together. And then, I draw, I draw and I draw again. It is like I can see it in my mind before it is made and clearly see it on the catwalk.

How important is research in your working process?

I need many things to nourish my inspiration: objects, images, stories and pieces of cloth. Everything that can make my mind travel and work. I continuously need to see new things, new places, to meet new people to listen to. At the same time, I need to be sure I can still count on old, steady things, things with a past and that already belonged to someone else. Things that have outlived time.

In 1999 Takada retired, and in 2003 Antonio Marras was made artistic director of Kenzo. Born in Sardinia in 1962, Marras had no formal schooling in fashion but developed such an interest in textiles that he convinced an entrepreneur from Rome to back him to create his first ready-to-wear collection in 1988. He made his haute couture debut under his own name in Paris in 1996 and his ready-to-wear debut in Milan in 1999. For Kenzo, Marras has developed the house's style by bringing together diverse references to communicate a contemporary design language. Fusing fashion with other art forms, Marras successfully brings a unique and modern vision to Kenzo.

Do you experience a 'eureka moment' when you know a design is working?

I am never content with my work. I have always felt I have to do better. As soon as the fashion show ends, my mind flies to the following one. I travel all the time, between my house in Sardinia, where I live and work, and Paris and Milan, both very important places for my work.

What is the best environment for you to work in?

My house is my haven, the place where I can design peacefully, while Paris is a pulsing city with new sensations and inspirations. Paris is maybe the only city where someone like me – always nostalgic, anxious and constantly in search of emotions – could live.

'I love flea markets, charity shops, old stuff sold in old stores and old fabric archives,' states Antonio Marras. For Kenzo's women's 'Alice in Wonderland' Spring/Summer 09 collection, the designer mixed different fabrics to create the romantic design signature that defines Kenzo.

According to Marras, 'Inspiration can be taken from everything. Photography, cinema, ballet, literature, painting, sculpture and modern art – for me, all of these have the same inspirational potential, and I do not tend to consider one of them superior to another.' These images are for the men's Autumn/Winter 09/10 'Russia' collection.

Design drawings with fabric indications for the women's Spring/Summer 09 collection.

Do you have sources of inspiration that you always revisit?

CHRIS BROOKE Vintage issues of *Vogue* are very inspiring, particularly looking at the contemporaries of the better-known designers of certain periods who perhaps didn't receive the same recognition. There are so many cutting techniques and details to be found that may not have been fully explored and it is exciting to use them in modern garments.

Does your design process involve photography, drawing or reading?

CHRIS BROOKE *Depending on the piece I'm working on, it may be more important to begin experimenting on the mannequin, as ideas can come about through simply pinning and stitching shapes together, ideas that wouldn't necessarily come from drawn work. And, then, the results are photographed so I can decide which parts are working and which aren't. I then mark the fabric and lie it flat to create the flat pattern.* BRUNO BASSO *It involves everything: photography, drawing, reading, visiting art galleries, listening to music, always looking for new technical resources and lots of Internet research. I don't usually make written notes as I prefer to express in the prints themselves the 'remembrance' of something rather than the observed image itself – it adds personal (and emotional) value to what you're doing.*

Is there a routine to your design process?

CHRIS BROOKE There is, but without it being a conscious process, because ultimately it is you as the designer who is making the choices and decisions. BRUNO BASSO I always prefer to think of it as an evolution. The research is always different and we always review the technical part.

Do you experience a 'eureka moment' when you know a design is working?

CHRIS BROOKE **Yes, always. It is the most satisfying when it ticks all the boxes: new, modern, flattering and innovative. There are times when a design works from a technical point of view in terms of a concept and is an achievement in terms of construction, but then when you look at it as a functional or flattering piece that a woman would want to wear it doesn't always work, and that can be frustrating.** BRUNO BASSO **Yes, always. It's difficult to describe but something clicks when a print is ready. I always squint and look at the print; if it works in the way I was initially expecting then it's ready. Sometimes, it's adventurous to take other decisions and directions in the middle of a process and you end up with something totally different from what you were imagining, but if it works, it works!**

How would you describe your design process?

CHRIS BROOKE *As we are a label of two people – myself for fashion and Bruno for graphic design and art – it is important for the garments to work in synergy with each other. Technology enables us to engineer the print to fit the garment with such precision; the possibilities are inspiring in themselves. It's an important role as a designer to move the industry forward.*

British-born Chris Brooke and Brazilian Bruno Basso are the designers behind Basso & Brooke. Brooke graduated in 1997 with an MA in womenswear from Central Saint Martins, while Basso was a student of journalism and advertising in Brazil, graduating in 2001 and subsequently working as a graphic designer. The Basso & Brooke label was conceived in 2003 and the design duo were the first ever winners of the Fashion Fringe award in 2004. Basso & Brooke are famed for their innovative use of digital print and colour in contemporary womenswear.

BASSO & BROOKE

What materials are essential to your working methods?

CHRIS BROOKE *A technical pencil. It's essential to keep putting ideas on paper without restraint. I tend not to have an eraser to hand as no matter how frivolous or impractical you think some ideas may be at the time, it is often those ideas that are the most interesting when you look back at hundreds of initial sketches.* BRUNO BASSO *Photoshop and the Internet.*

What is the most enjoyable part of designing for you?

CHRIS BROOKE The most enjoyable part is solving the problem of how to create the shape or cut in the most interesting manner. It is important to understand the technicalities of pattern cutting and what is possible with fabric. Most designers pass this process on to a pattern cutter, but the journey of getting what you want can often reveal interesting and new ideas. The most difficult thing is when you know there is a fantastic idea there, but find it almost impossible to execute in a way that works in all dimensions. BRUNO BASSO I love the initial research and the completion on the catwalk. The day-by-day transformation from one to the other is the most difficult and challenging part, but it's as enjoyable.

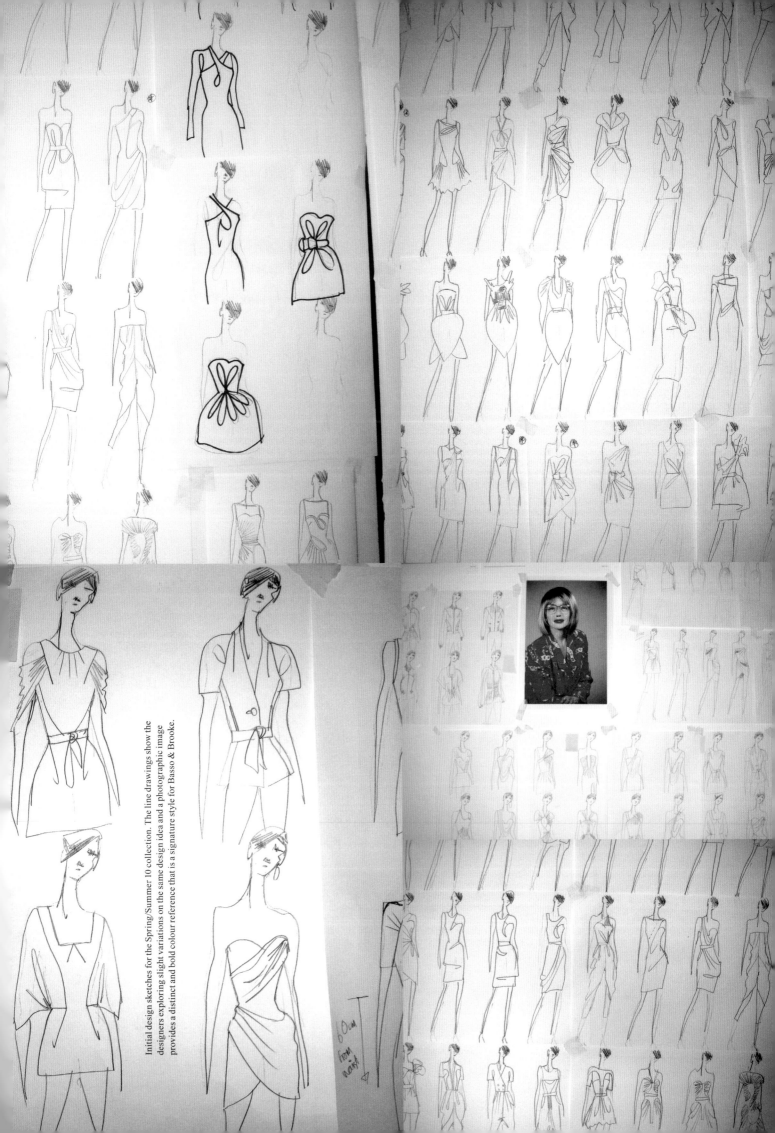

Initial design sketches for the Spring/Summer 10 collection. The line drawings show the designers exploring slight variations on the same design idea and a photographic image provides a distinct and bold colour reference that is a signature style for Basso & Brooke.

60cm
From wad

An experiment for a basket-weave-inspired tucking technique on a dress for the Spring/Summer 09 collection. The image below the dress indicates the original source of inspiration: a photograph of basket weave.

cut in one piece to give fit & illusion of basket weave.

oversized lattice smocking

TOP — Fabric is draped on the stand and photographed during toile development for a garment in the Spring/Summer 09 collection. **BOTTOM** — First the garment is constructed using a toile or prototype fabric before it is constructed in the real fabric. The Japanese-inspired dress is from the Spring/Summer 09 collection.

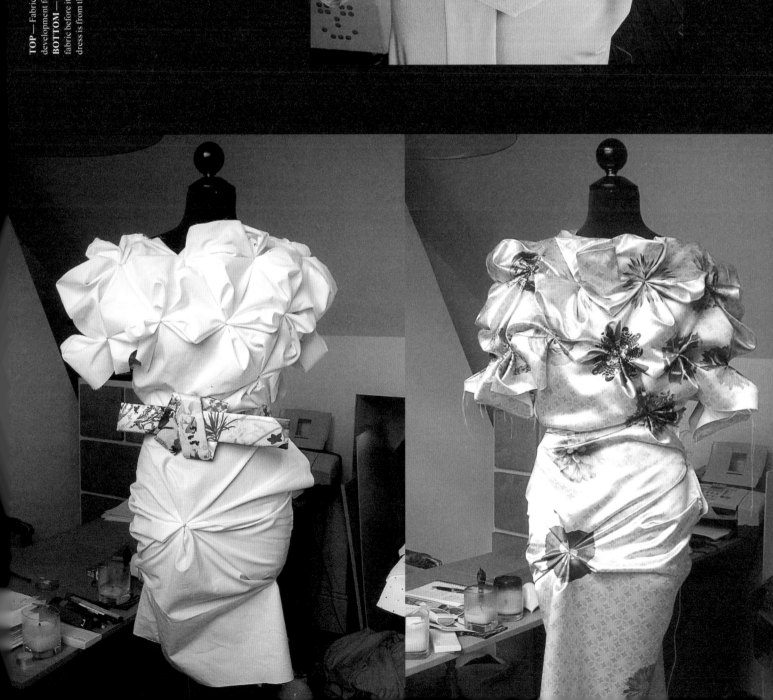

BLAAK

Sachiko Okada and Aaron Sharif are the design team behind London-based label Blaak. Both studied at Central Saint Martins before forming Blaak in 1998. The concept behind the label was developed through reflection on the emotions aroused by the colour black. The designers explore cutting and tailoring techniques and their fabric choice communicates the importance of tactility in their designs, enabling them to present sensuous fabrics with a masculine aesthetic.

How important is research in your working process?

AARON SHARIF It's more of a mental research. A dialogue about things that we remember and want to see again and attitudes that felt right.

SACHIKO OKADA Research is the backbone of the collection. Not necessarily just visual research but also collecting and memorizing feelings, situations, emotions caused by something. This information goes through our system and becomes a more tangible theme. Research becomes less subconscious from this point.

What materials are essential to your working methods?

AARON SHARIF I've found recently that I want to challenge the way I put my ideas to paper. For Autumn/Winter 08/09, I found it was more comfortable working with my eyes closed. This freed me from my own constraints of presenting my ideas. For Spring/ Summer 10, I decided to work more with my left hand. As I'm naturally right-handed, this slowed down my working process, but allowed a greater attention to thought and detail. In a strange way it also brought out a more vulnerable side to my work.

What is the most enjoyable part of designing for you?

AARON SHARIF Every process has triumphs. Having ideas and seeing them work or not. Taking the process from a discussion to a sketch and then choosing fabric and deadlines.

SACHIKO OKADA It's good when ideas exceed the imagination. The difficult part is when we have to commit to fabrics. From this point on, it becomes a concrete reality and the process becomes more practical and less abstract.

What is the best environment for you to work in?

AARON SHARIF *I can work anywhere, no conditions.*

SACHIKO OKADA *I can have an idea anywhere; executing the idea is best done at the studio.*

Does your design process involve photography, drawing or reading?

AARON SHARIF Our approach is more of a holistic one; by this I mean it involves everything. SACHIKO OKADA It depends on the season. Photography, drawing and reading are all good for showing yourself what is forming in your mind. You'd only take a picture of a subject that left a strong impression on you. Reading is the same. It's a good gateway to realizing what you are feeling.

What fuels your design ideas?

AARON SHARIF **Deadlines are always the best fuel and driving force. You can achieve so much when you have to finish.**

SACHIKO OKADA **The clothes that we design. So, the main subject is the people. To observe and to discover aspects of people, whether in a book or in reality, is important.**

How would you describe your design process?

AARON SHARIF *It starts off slowly and in a reassured way and then speeds up to the point that it takes over. It never starts off definitely, meaning each step influences the next and takes it to a higher conclusion.* SACHIKO OKADA *It's like trying to put a jigsaw image together. Each piece is necessary for any other piece to exist. As more and more pieces come together, you see the bigger picture.*

How does your research and design work evolve from 2D to 3D?

SACHIKO OKADA When I have an idea in my head, it's 3D. Trying to put a three-dimensional idea on to paper is not the easiest thing. I always feel that what I see in my head is better than what I see on the paper in front of me. In a way, this frustration becomes a strong driving force to pursue ideas into reality.

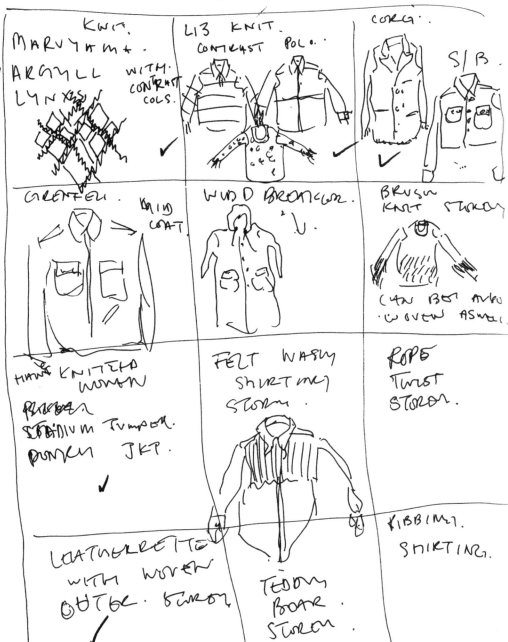

BOTTOM LEFT — A design sketch for a contrast Glencheck and dogstooth wool gauze suit for the Autumn/Winter 09/10 'Man vs Machine' collection. The drawing demonstrates the importance of the texture of the fabrics.
BOTTOM RIGHT — A drawing for a contrasting asymmetric mohair knitted pullover, for the Autumn/Winter 09/10 'Man vs Machine' collection.

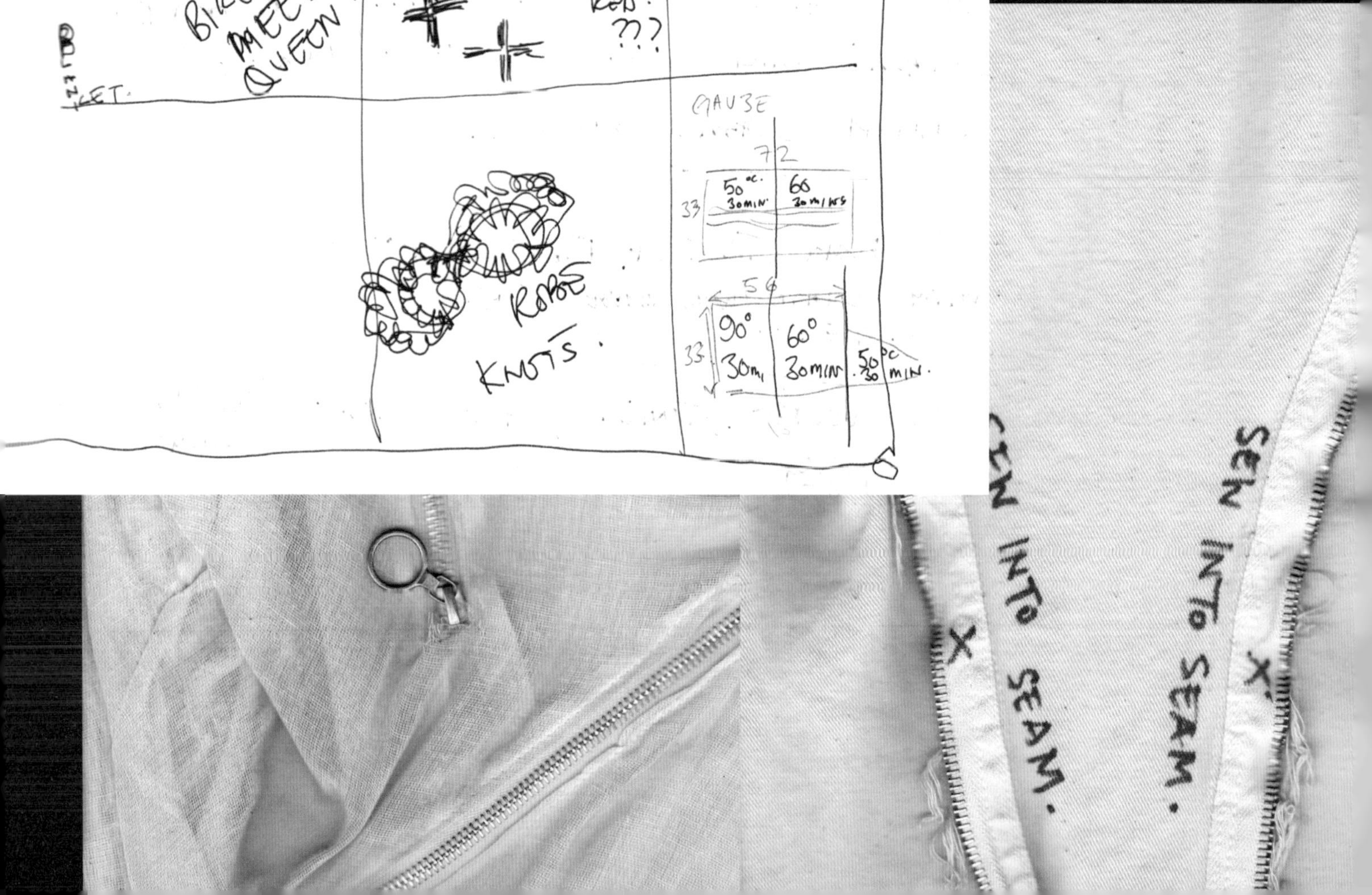

EDWARD LOW
 teddy BOY.

JERSON SHIRTING. PADDED. STORY.	BONDAGE. STORY. STUDDED FELT.	STUDDED VELVET.
SOFT. TAILORING. SOFT.	WOVEN. HOODY JOGGING. STORY	JERSON TAILORING. STORY. ???
HORSE BLANKET?	QUILTON. WARNY KUBER BIKER MEETS QUEEN	HAND DRAWN HOUND. TOOTH, BLK. x RED ???	FLOATING SEAM

ROPE KNOTS.

GAUSE

72

33	50 °C. 30MIN.	60 30 M/HS

56

33	90° 30M	60° 30MIN	50 °C 30 MIN.

SEN INTO SEAM.
X
SEN INTO SEAM.
X

TOP — Initial ideas for the Autumn/Winter 09/10 collection. The design notes show how the designers describe the techniques and fabrics that will be used in the collection.

BOTTOM — Winter 08/09 'Buffalo Soldier' collection. Instructions for manufacture are written on the prototype garment in red ink.

FELT
SHIRT
WITH
BLUE
STRIPE

FRONT.

Design drawing of a contrasting felt stripe shirt and raw-cut wool cycling shorts for the Autumn/
Winter 09/10 'Man vs Machine' collection. The drawing suggests the mood of the collection.

A 'Peace Dove' foil-print T-shirt design for the
Autumn/Winter 08/09 'Buffalo Soldier' collection.

BORA AKSU

Turkish Bora Aksu graduated from Central Saint Martins in 2002. The following year he made his catwalk debut during the off-schedule shows at London Fashion Week, as a result of which he received the Top Shop New Generation Award. Aksu's signature style is described as romanticism with a darker edge. His clothes are inherently modern, fusing complex cutting techniques with minimal seaming and mixing soft and stiff fabrics with delicate details.

How important is research in your working process?
The research process is very important if it is naturally progressed. In other words, it needs to be exciting and enjoyable. I do like the research process especially when floating ideas start to become concrete design tools. It can be an idea, a thought, something that I might have started thinking a season before.

Do you have sources of inspiration that you always revisit?
I do like contrasts a lot. I find it interesting how contrasts work so well together. And, I usually draw inspiration from personal memories. With regard to revisited sources, I would say the 1970s punk era, the late Edwardian period and everyday items such as tea towels. I am always drawn to movies, colours and styling from the 1970s. There's a naive innocence but also a strange awakening that you find in many movies from this period and I think the colours reflect that really well.

Is there a specific time of day when you are most creative?
I think it's always at night. During the day, it's more about resolving ideas and dealing with everyday stuff and the studio is always full of people. But at night I can focus and have clear ideas.

Does your design process involve photography, drawing or reading?
I try not to put any limits on my design process. Inspiration is something that needs to move freely.

What is the most enjoyable part of designing for you?
I enjoy sketching a lot, but I also enjoy the translation process. It's amazing how ideas actually change when you apply them to fabrics. I like the evolution from 2D ideas to 3D objects. Also, there are always accidental results in this process, which sometimes turn into excellent design ideas.

What materials are essential to your working methods?
Whether I am in my studio or outside, I need to have loads of white A4 paper with 0.5 pencils.

How would you describe your design process?
My design process is a visual evolution that blends with many different elements. It is important to know your own design language.

An illustration from Bora Aksu's sketchbook for the Autumn/Winter 09/10 collection. The illustration portrays the Victorian influences within the collection along with the nomadic references. It was made to demonstrate the mood of the collection and is entitled 'Picnic at Hanging Rock'.

OPPOSITE — This is Bora Aksu's research and colour reference for the Autumn/Winter 08/09 collection. The different shades of reds are derived from colour experiments and are kept as a reference point.

Preparation work for the Autumn/Winter 08/09 collection. The Polaroid photographs are from the fittings for the same collection.

Bora Aksu's sketchbook contains experimental work for the Autumn/Winter 09/10 collection. The idea was to explore the possibilities of corset laces and to see the different design ideas develop through these experiments. The Polaroids show the experimental work that took place on the stand and the illustration reveals what the designer was aiming to achieve.

BOUDICCA

Zowie Broach and Brian Kirkby graduated from Middlesex University and went into partnership to create Boudicca in 1997. Named in honour of the Celtic warrior queen, Boudicca is more of an art project than a fashion line. Boudicca creates beautiful clothes that are impeccably cut and non-conformist. The designers explore the balance between edginess and femininity through their highly stylized and refined collections.

How would you describe your design process?

We plan to create something invisible. Another dimension. Science and technology sit on the edge of many new areas, which is extremely invigorating and exciting as far as all our futures are concerned. When this technology is partnered with ideas and creative spirit then and only then will it create a new marvel for mankind. That is the area, the dimension, that we are looking to work within, come closer to.

What fuels your design ideas?

Boudicca is a set of tensions that climbs in and out of the masculine and the feminine, history and the future, tailing all thoughts and that when brought together forms a new language that defines itself in the moment. 'Now' we are living in a post-modernist glitch that we must endeavour to break out of, and move towards a neo-modernism, with new ideology taking into account our experiences of the world we live in. We must with all our heart and soul stop looking backwards for nostalgia, which as we all know is comfortable and easy to understand.

An abstract photographic reference image by Boudicca informed work created for the Arnhem Fashion Biennale in 2009.

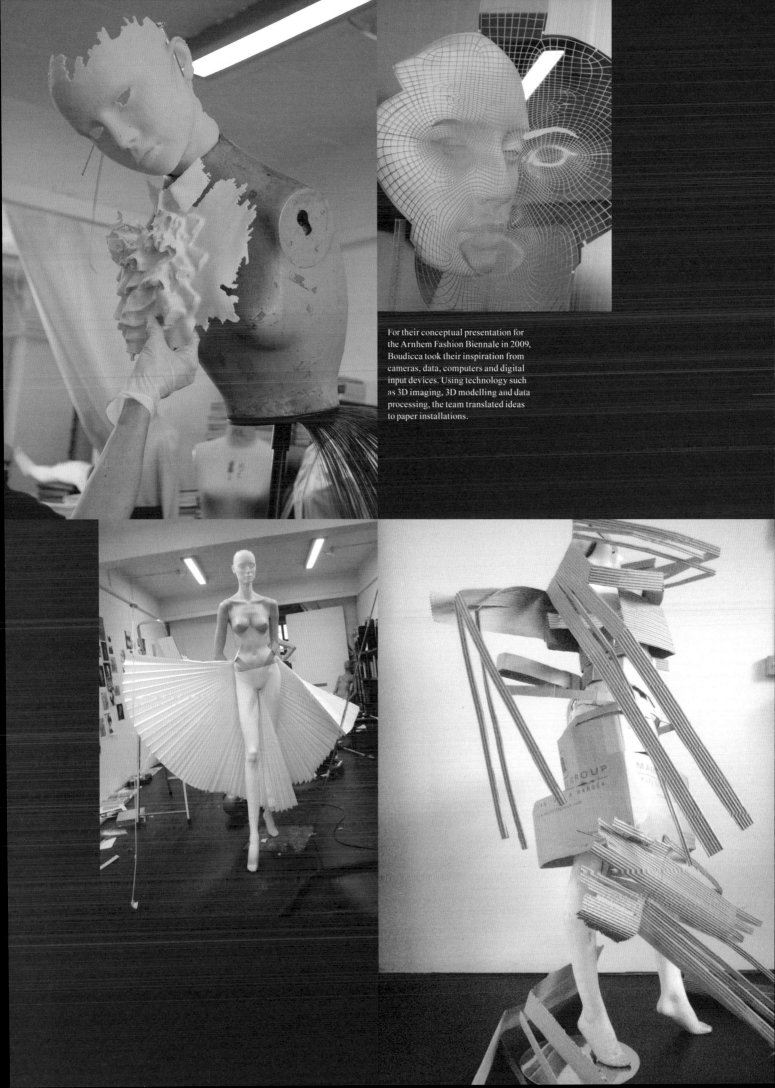

For their conceptual presentation for the Arnhem Fashion Biennale in 2009, Boudicca took their inspiration from cameras, data, computers and digital input devices. Using technology such as 3D imaging, 3D modelling and data processing, the team translated ideas to paper installations.

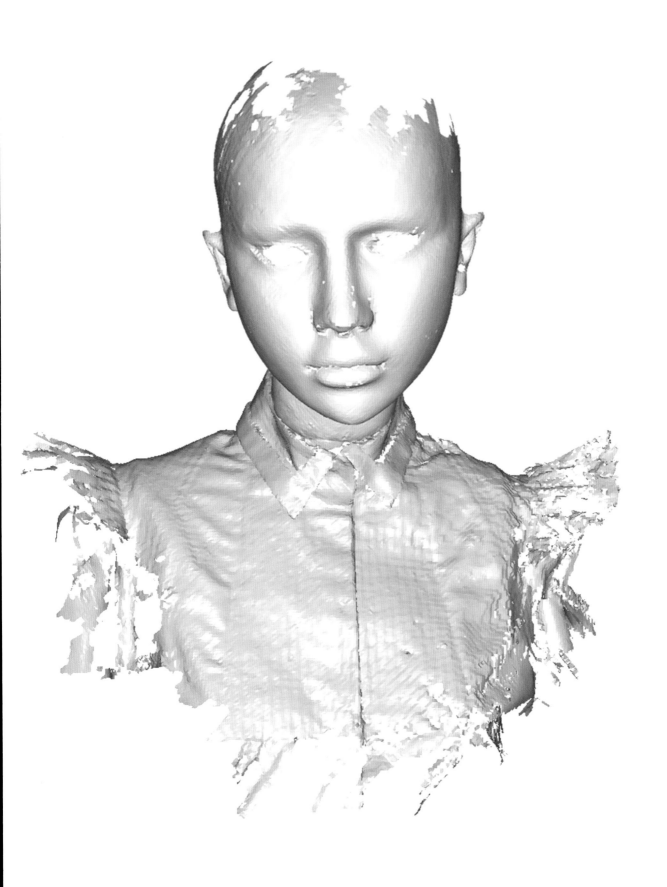

An output image – 'Mapped Face' – for the Arnhem Fashion Biennale in 2009 illustrates Boudicca's progressive and contemporary approach to fashion presentation.

What materials are essential to your working methods?

I don't need specific materials, more like a specific state of mind. Something between panic, not caring and the knowledge that I have always got it done and that I will also do so this time.

What is the most enjoyable part of designing for you?

I love getting into the 'flow'. This usually involves insomnia, solitude and listening to the same piece of music for hours. I have a love-hate relationship with putting my ideas on paper so they mirror exactly what's in my head, often to the extent that I either start cutting and making straight away or I spend eons on a detailed drawing.

Born in Gießen, Germany, Carola Euler studied tailoring in her hometown before moving to London in 1999. She graduated from Central Saint Martins in 2005 and launched her own menswear collection as part of the Fashion East MAN showcase in September 2006 during London Fashion Week. Euler makes clothes that link humour and integrity. Her designs are based on sharp angles, clean lines and complex details.

Do you have sources of inspiration that you always revisit?

Creatively, I think I've always been inspired by how the people in the American West dress, though I've never been there. It's a kind of 'non-style'. I love Richard Avedon's portraits of these really intense-looking but normal people. They manage to wear a pair of jeans and a jumper and look completely styled. It's like Tesco-supermarket-type clothes but they look amazing. I think this is always the underlying idea for me, though I then introduce a technical part and try to make something tricky look simple. I make it harder for myself, trying to make it appear 'easy'.

CAROLA EULER

What are your sources of inspiration?

Everything really, but it's the film in my head that develops out of all the impressions I have gathered in-between collections that forms my vision. I often look at older work of mine and realize that there's a natural progression. I don't worry that much about not having an idea or being uninspired. It's the balancing of everything that is the biggest headache and the most fun.

Does your design process involve photography, drawing or reading?

It involves all three, but mostly in retrospect. At the time when I took that picture, made that drawing or read that piece I didn't know it would be part of my research. My research always ends up being a collection of things I have already produced or collected before with no specific intent. The major part of my design process happens in my head.

What fuels your design ideas?

The pure fear of knowing that if I don't start now I won't get it done on time. It works very much like accelerating at full throttle and then finally releasing the handbrake. When I know decisions have to come fast, I go with my gut feeling, which I have learned to trust.

What is the best environment for you to work in?

My bed when I am half asleep, under the shower when I don't have a pen, on public transport with a Walkman and while driving. Anything but at my desk.

How important is research in your working process?

I don't really set a time aside for research, but I take time if I need it. It's kind of like snacking when you get hungry.

How would you describe your design process?

It's ongoing. Usually, I already know the starting point of the following collection while I am working on the current one. It tends to be a 'branch' that couldn't be included but keeps on growing independently.

Is there a specific time of day when you are most creative?

At night. I didn't know that people were actually creative at any other time of day.

Do you experience a 'eureka moment' when you know a design is working?

Absolutely. I get completely overexcited and take the rest of the day off.

1 X
2
3 X
4 X
5 X
6
6 X
7 X

black mesh

black mesh

white leather

black mesh/
poss. no cap

unlined 2/cotage.
no shoulder pads

medical coat fabric
dyed grey

+ medical coat
frame for
waistcoat

SHIRT # ①

WHITE

& 1+ or
Skeleton +
T-shirt

JERSEY
BELOW +
SHOWING
SKELETON

SLIGHTLY
PADDED
EPAULETTES

LIGHTLY
PADDED
TROUSER
(ENTIRE)

COAT ✓

DOUBLE
STRAPS
ON
SLEEVES

BIG CUP

TRIM PANTS

- STAY CREASE
- 1 BACK POCKET
RIGHT SIDE

CORDUROY
TROUSERS

TROUSER

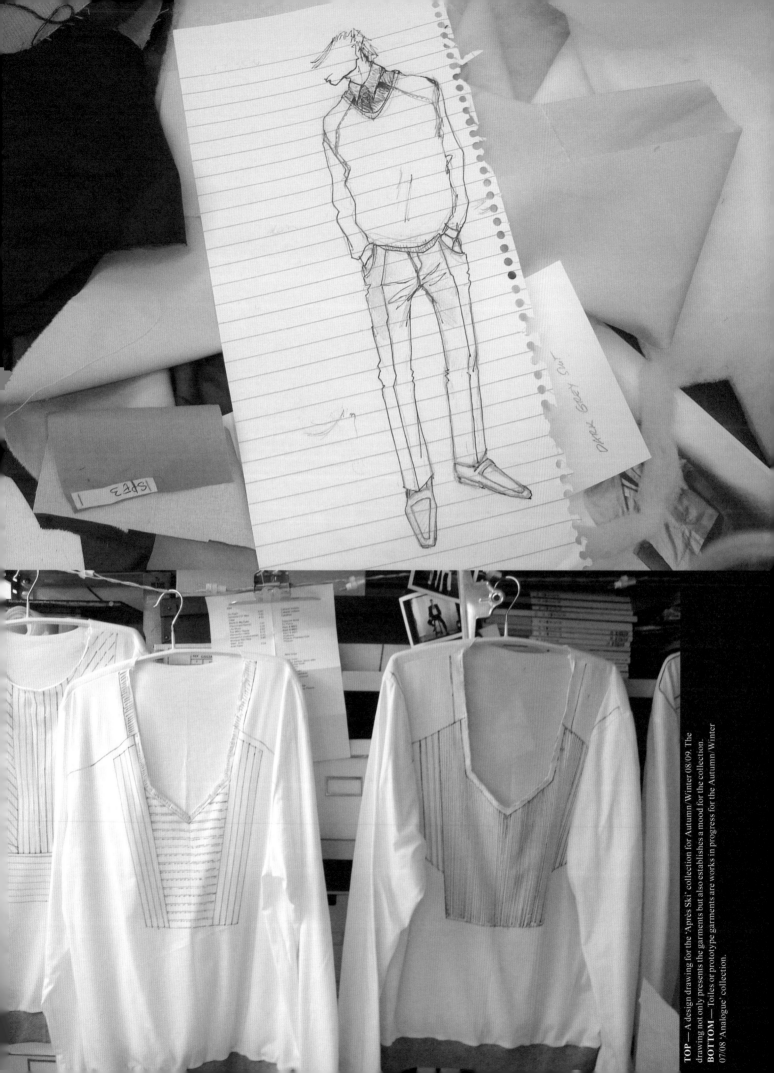

TOP — A design drawing for the 'Après Ski' collection for Autumn/Winter 08/09. The drawing not only presents the garments but also establishes a mood for the collection.
BOTTOM — Toiles or prototype garments are works in progress for the Autumn/Winter 07/08 'Analogue' collection.

Is there a specific time of day when you are most creative?

I like to get up at 6am and work in my leopard-print dressing gown. The studio is quiet. Sometimes I'll put on some horrendous 1980s music and dance while I work.

What fuels your design ideas?

I'm a natural researcher – I was always the annoying child asking too many questions, and I am a visual consumer. I'm at my happiest on my own rummaging through dirty flea markets or dark museum archives.

Do you have sources of inspiration that you always revisit?

I always turn to [German photographer] August Sander's Citizens of the Twentieth Century, *obscure books on uniform around the world, war films that come free with the* Daily Mail, *pictures of men from all eras in various states of dress (it's also interesting to see how people wear garments and how styling can inspire design) and music. My work definitely comes from quite an emotional place, and music is integral to that. There's a soundtrack to each season.*

What materials are essential to your working methods?

A Moleskin diary comes with me everywhere and a 0.7 black gel pen. I use a very particular rubber from Muji when pattern cutting and, of course, a mechanical pencil, 0.5 lead.

How important is research in your working process?

Research is an integral part. A wise man once said to me, 'fashion does not come from fashion', and it's so true. I like to start by going to the flea markets in Paris while I'm there for sales and doing garment research. I'm fascinated by the way garments are constructed and how this can inform the design.

Menswear designer Carolyn Massey graduated from the Royal College of Art in London in 2005. She started her own label in 2006, with a focus on beautifully refined detailing and exquisite fabrics. Her collections explore the notion of 'what it is to be a gentleman' and how this can be communicated through contemporary clothing.

What is the most enjoyable part of designing for you?

I'm desperately in love with all of it. There are parts of the process that I am better at than others, but you learn what tasks are better to delegate and what you should keep hold of. I think when you become so obsessed with something it can be terribly unhealthy, but there's also something really seductive about that.

How would you describe your design process?

It's a mixture of order and disorder. I'm conscious that I can get visually bored quite easily, so it's a mix of almost knowing which pieces I want in the edit from the start and designing something two weeks before the show and working like crazy to get it realized in time. There's something quite torturous about this process but I quite like that.

What is the best environment for you to work in?

I think I'm always working, always gathering ideas. When you work in a visual medium, you can't help this. My studio is the best environment.

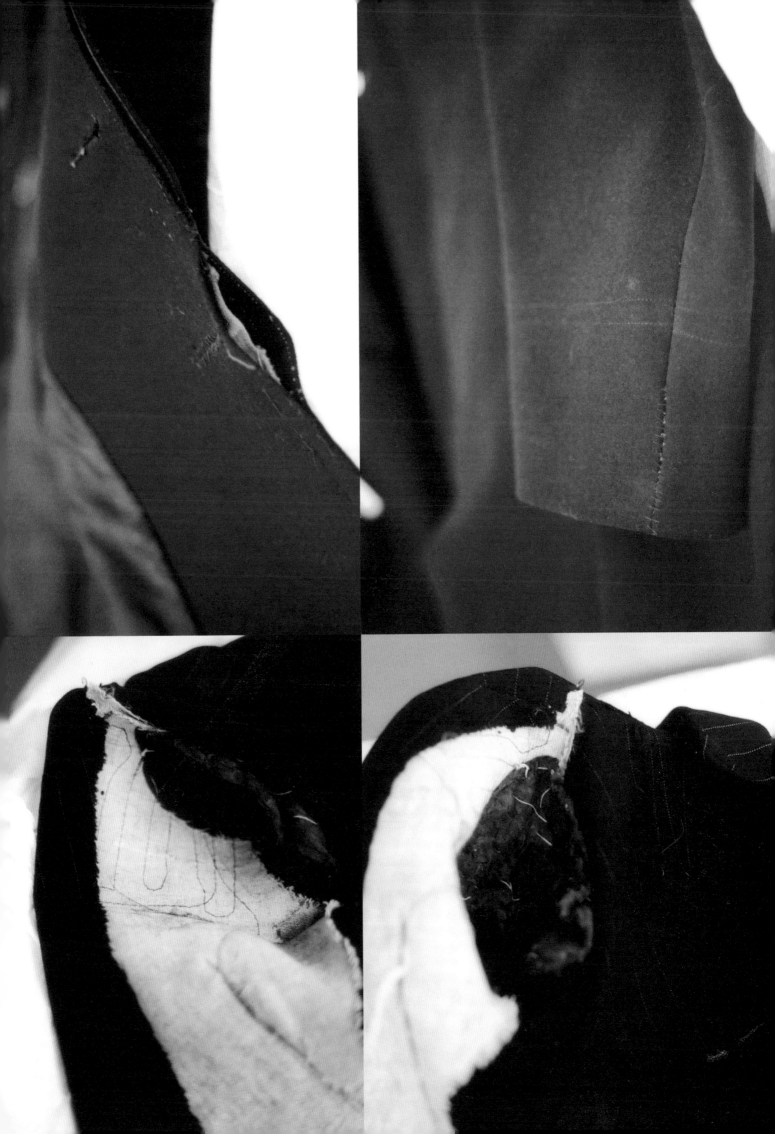

TOP — The designer's desk as at the design stage of the Autumn/Winter 09/10 collection, showing a diverse range of references and inspiration.
BOTTOM LEFT — An image of a rose shot by Chris Brooks and given to Carolyn Massey. It is used as an inspirational reference for future collections.
BOTTOM RIGHT — Photograph of Les Deux Garçons shooting in Paris for the Autumn/Winter 07/08 look book. Model Dan Sharpe.

An image of a backstage board that was hung at the end of a model's (Pawel) rail for the Autumn/Winter 09/10 show. The board shows how the garments should be worn and also the appropriate accessories.

PAGE 53 — Close-up photographs of the construction of a coat in the archives at The Museum of London, taken for research for the Autumn/Winter 09/10 collection. By studying historical garments Carolyn Massey is inspired by their function and construction.

Does your design process involve photography, drawing or reading?

We use all of those things. We both work in slightly different ways: Dorothee prefers to draw and make toiles, while I work more with collage, on the computer and on the knitting machine.

Our design process has evolved over the last two years of working together. We have various stages whereby we work either individually or together on the collection. We have different skills, so we often concentrate on different areas. I love graphic pattern and knit techniques, so I tend to focus more on these aspects, while Dorothee specializes in pattern cutting, garment construction and working with the factories.

COOPERATIVE DESIGNS

Annalisa Dunn and Dorothee Hagemann met on the MA in Fashion Knitwear at Central Saint Martins in 2007. Upon graduation they joined forces to create Cooperative Designs. Their knitwear collections specialize in strong graphics, stripes and multilayered knits.

How important is research in your working process?

It plays an incredibly important part. We start by looking around: at people on the street, at our friends, magazines, films and blogs. Once we feel inspired we go to the library and look at designers, photographers, graphics, furniture, anything we feel stimulated by. We also spend time researching traditional knit techniques and patterns, which we combine with modern quirky elements.

Is there a routine to your design process?

We research individually, then come together and discuss themes for each new collection. We then design individually again, using a mixture of sketches, collages and computer techniques to illustrate and develop the designs. We source yarns and fabrics and consult with our factories to see if they can produce the new techniques. The next stage is making toiles, which can take days or weeks to get right for each design. Once the toiles have been finalized, a line-up of designs is created to give an overview of the collection. We analyse the collection constantly, in terms of a catwalk show, a showroom collection, and in terms of the final customers – how wearable, affordable and desirable the collection is. It is a real challenge to get everything right. Each season we learn more and more about the process.

What is the best environment for you to work in?
We have a studio where we work. Evenings and weekends are great, when it is a little quieter and we can focus better.

What is the most enjoyable part of designing for you?

Coming up with ideas and broad research is really fun. Editing the ideas down and being strict and analytical is challenging. Time and money provide extra restrictions. It can be frustrating to realize an idea is unaffordable, but finding a way to work around that can be very rewarding.

What fuels your design ideas?

A constant desire to improve and develop from where we are. We always spend time analysing our previous collections and identifying areas we need to develop in order to move forward. Our typical references include the Bauhaus, constructivism and traditional knit techniques.

BACK IMAGE — As knitwear is the core element of Cooperative Designs' work, swatches are often used as the starting point for the garment designs. This hand-knit swatch of marled lambswool with striped cut-jersey intarsia was used to inform the Autumn/Winter 08/09 collection.

FRONT IMAGE — In their studio, the designers dressed a hoover and a broom in a dress from their Autumn/Winter 08/09 collection. The Polaroid was used to develop their concept identity and was sent to the press and buyers. Photographed by Cooperative Designs.

Design collages for the Autumn/Winter 09/10 collection. As oversized texture is integral to its collection, the designers used knit samples as collage on their design drawings, allowing them to experiment with proportion and silhouette.

Design for a graphic knit concept for the Spring/Summer 09 collection.

Do you have sources of inspiration that you always revisit?

I love words. One word can change and challenge everything for me. I would say that the names of my collections are like a gang; that's why I have parts to each collection, for example, 'WIZARD', 'AWISC' (a wolf in sheep's clothing), 'WIZARD V MACHINE'.

How important is research in your working process?

Research can be a word, a picture or twenty pictures – it's whatever opens your head and gets you.

DERYCK WALKER

Deryck Walker was born in Scotland, remaining there to study Fashion and Textiles at Glasgow School of Art. On graduation, he moved to London to work for such designers as Boudicca and Robert Cary-Williams. Following a time in Milan working for Versace, Walker returned to London in 2004 to launch his menswear collection, which was sold in Dover Street Market. In 2008, he presented his first womenswear collection. Walker's collections are often based on contrasts: 'I always like a man to be a man, but I do like to use a little bit of feminine influence'.

What is the best environment for you to work in?

I like being in the studio working with the team, but I do like a bit of solitude. Things can change so much if you don't get some clarity for yourself. Also I like to be in a place where you suddenly feel you could soak it up like a sponge. I felt like this when I went to Japan for the first time – memory overload!!

Is there a specific time of day when you are most creative?

It is usually when people leave the studio in the evening. I love to sweep the floor and tidy up myself and then go over what has happened that day.

What fuels your design ideas?

I really like finding good books. When working on 'ORACLE', I really got into Francis Bacon. The books I bought were a valuable source; also [filmmaker] John Maybury's account of Bacon's life was great to look at.

What does your research entail?

My research involves everything from a chewing-gum wrapper to a song. When I was producing the 'ORACLE' collection I was working with lots of transparency, so sweet wrappers to shower curtains got me thinking.

How would you describe your design process?

I don't know if I have a process that I stick to every season, so the best way for me to describe it is that it changes all the time, depending on what I am inspired by.

Is there a routine to your design process?

I can start making toiles and this takes a couple of days to get into, especially when I am cutting a new pattern. Another way would be to go straight ahead and make something. I think my method is very fluid in the sense that I just go with it; I try not to think about it too much.

TOILE : VENTRILR COAT

EFGH.

VENTRILR COAT

LMNUVW J

XYZRSTOP

STRL COAT.
MMRTRIC

QHIJKABC

LMNDEFGHI

CLASSIC SUIT

PAGE 61 & BELOW — For his Spring/Summer 08 collection entitled 'Information', Deryck Walker took inspiration from 1940s tailoring and 1950s youth culture. The working concept boards unite Walker's influences and include typography, design sketches, working toiles, Polaroids, fabric swatches and imagery.

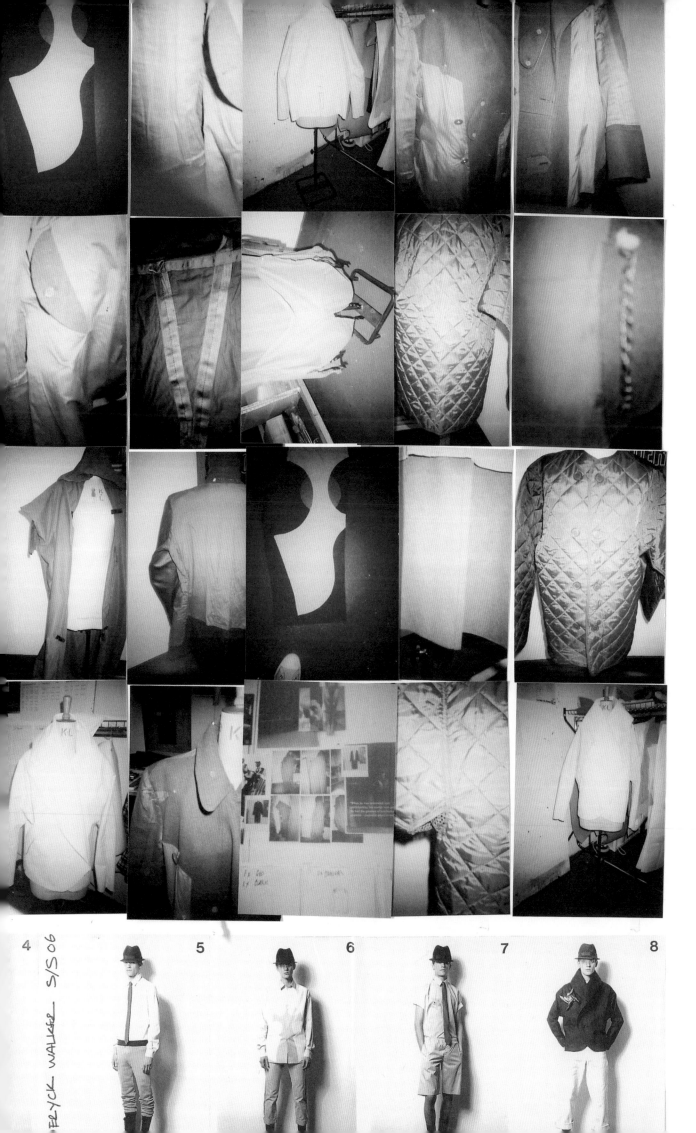

Photographs taken to inspire the 'MACHINE' collection for Spring/Summer 06. Walker explores the construction of vintage garments. The line-up at the bottom of the board illustrates the final styled garments.

4   5   6   7   8

ERYCK WALKER S/S 06

Is there a routine to your design process?

I always try to challenge the limits of what's possible, whether that be through using the technology of a factory or the skills of a tiny atelier, a machine or the hands of an artisan. My design approach combines the limits of technology today with the soul of all that has preceded us.

What materials are essential to your working methods?

A bad workman blames his tools; it is more a question of spirit than materials. A free mind, heart and the enthusiasm of a great team will always remain essential.

Do you have sources of inspiration that you always revisit?

I remain fascinated by the past, by history and the history of fashion. All of my work is rooted in this appreciation of what has been and gone. It is not to mimic something that's already happened, but more to revisit certain elements with a contemporary vision. A modern approach to design is, for me, the space between an object from another time and its reinterpretation. Inspiration can strike in a flash at any time, from anywhere and involve the reassessment of anything.

What is the most enjoyable part of designing for you?

I prefer to live, see and enjoy the entire process as a whole, focusing on one part no matter how pleasant or unpleasant is futile for me.

Does your design process involve photography, drawing or reading?

The answer to your question would be 'all of the above', and to be honest, any one or all of them can take me on a journey. Since I started designing I have always used elements from a multitude of sources: music, books, art and photography. The final product, however, what you see on the catwalk, is not a direct translation of these influences but more of a personal interpretation.

Do you experience a 'eureka moment' when you know a design is working?
Of course, it is more or less our drug.

DRIES VAN NOTEN

Is there a specific time of day when you are most creative?
No, I am pretty even throughout the day.

Born in Antwerp, Belgium, in 1958, Dries Van Noten studied at Antwerp Royal Academy of Fine Arts, and in 1985 created his own label. The following year, as part of the influential 'Antwerp Six', he showed his collection in London, which launched Van Noten's international career. In 1988, Van Noten received the Award of the Flemish Community for his work. During the same year, he opened a boutique in Antwerp and started selling his clothes in Japan. He debuted his menswear collection in Paris in 1991 and his women's line in 1993. Dries Van Noten's designs are characterized by his ability to take beautiful fabrics, colours and prints and create wearable and practical garments. His clothes are both pared down and sophisticated. Incorporating classical ideas into contemporary designs, Van Noten produces clothes that transcend seasonal trends and are distinct in their refined appeal.

Do you have a team that is involved in the design process? If so, what do they do?
Of course, fashion is essentially a collaborative process and I am lucky to have a stable team of individualists who complement, share and push my creative horizons.

How would you describe your design process?
I don't necessarily have one assigned design process per se. I guess one of the multitude of different ways that I begin a collection is to take something that I do not find immediately alluring and transform it into something beautiful or at least challenging. For example, mauve has never been my favourite colour, yet my disdain for the tone forced me to create a collection mainly in mauve. In much the same way, colours that don't necessarily look good knitted or in wool may possibly turn out beautifully when executed in mat silk. By changing a base fabric, material or support you can end up with a completely different message, and this shift in viewpoint can spawn the beginning of an entire collection.

How important is research in your working process?
Fabric is my starting point. I'm known predominantly for colour, prints and embroidery – normally the more they clash, the more I like it. Fabrics give me my initial inspiration and represent, for the most part, the essence of what my collections look like.

Does your design process involve photography, drawing or reading?

We read, we write and we sketch. Our design process involves the lives we lead. So in so far as we read and look at pictures, yes, everything inspires us. We sketch every season all the looks; that is part of our design process.

DUCKIE BROWN

New York-based menswear label Duckie Brown is designed by Steven Cox and Daniel Silver. Cox used to be a designer at Tommy Hilfiger, while Silver worked as a daytime TV producer. Together they create quirky clothes that are simultaneously elegant and dishevelled. Core to all their collections is an emphasis on the shoulder; the tailored jacket and tailored coat are the starting points for all their ideas. In 2006, Duckie Brown was nominated for the Perry Ellis New Menswear Award, given by the Council of Fashion Designers of America (CFDA).

Do you have sources of inspiration that you always revisit?

Our inspiration comes from the lives we lead and includes everything we encounter. There are a few constants in every collection: we are always revisiting Charlie Chaplin and Ray Petri.

How would you describe your design process?

It starts from our guts and our minds. We have a strong feeling of what we are going to do and then proceed. We sketch in sketchbooks or sketch anywhere on anything. Writing in our sketchbooks has become a very important part of the design process.

What materials are essential to your working methods?
A Moleskin sketchbook, a Staedtler Mars Lumograph 2B pencil, a seven-inch metal ruler, a Staedtler rubber and Bienfang translucent sketch paper.

What is the most enjoyable part of designing for you?

It's the most wonderful, frightening, exciting process in the world. At times it is effortless and at other times just hard work.

Do you experience a 'eureka moment' when you know a design is working?
Yes. You just know deep inside your guts when it's right.

How important is research in your working process?

We are always researching new mills and new factories. As far as the collection goes, we never reference the past – it's always about looking forward. We are forever researching, we never stop.

Two design drawings from the Spring/Summer 10 collection. On the left, a funnel-neck check bomber jacket, khaki cotton asymmetrical shorts and a vivid blue chiffon shirt. On the right, a tweed double-breasted jacket, a striped chiffon shirt and basket-weave cotton shorts.

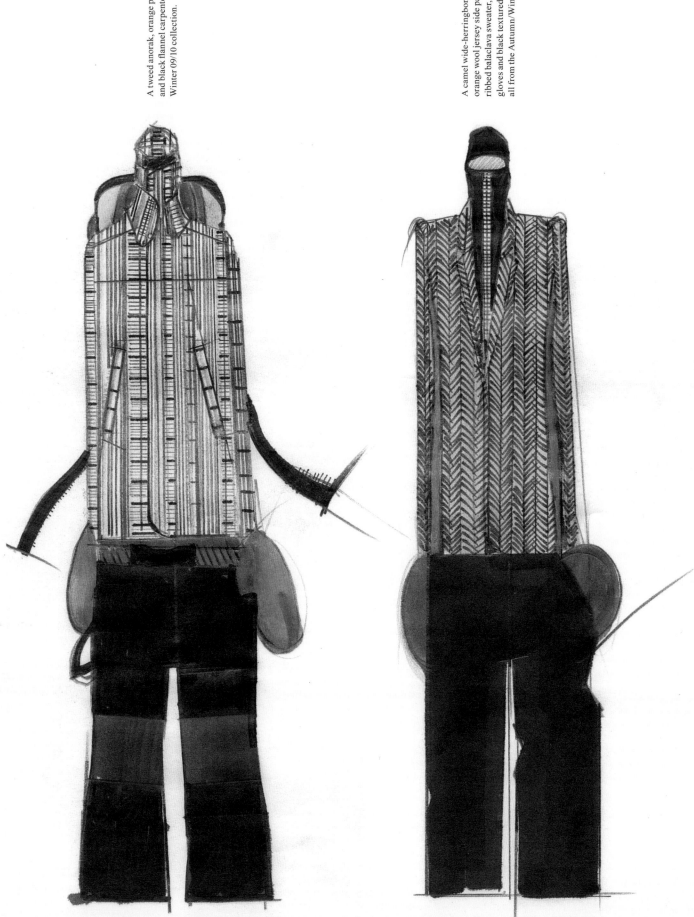

A tweed anorak, orange puffy suede gloves, a backpack and black flannel carpenter trousers from the Autumn/ Winter 09/10 collection.

A camel wide-herringbone wool one-button jacket with orange wool jersey side panels, a black merino-wool ribbed balaclava sweater, black nylon padded circular gloves and black textured-nylon padded-knee trousers, all from the Autumn/Winter 09/10 collection.

How would you describe your design process?

The design process at E. Tautz is genuinely a collective effort. There are three of us who are intimately involved, and at least five others whose advice we seek and whose skills we call upon. For us, the process usually starts with an idea of a particular character in a particular place, someone who we feel embodies the Tautz idea of men's elegance. For the season just gone, we started with an image of the Duke of Windsor stepping on to a sailing dinghy in Majorca. He's wearing a panama hat, a pair of rather short shorts, a pair of espadrilles and is carrying a set of bagpipes.

E. TAUTZ

Patrick Grant, owner of Savile Row's Norton & Sons, relaunched the historic sporting and military label E. Tautz as a ready-to-wear collection in 2009. E. Tautz had originally dressed such figures as Winston Churchill, Edward VII and Cary Grant, with a focus on substance and durability rather than showy fabrics. The garments are built to be part of a carefully assembled wardrobe of clothes to be passed from generation to generation.

How important is research in your working process?

Research is fundamental to the way we begin the process of assembling our collections. From our starting idea, we begin the task of gathering a collection of images, both historical and contemporary, that resonate with our central idea. Claire, James and I trawl through the photo archives. We use our own small library, the libraries at the fashion colleges and the public libraries, and we draw upon the collections of a couple of private museums that are a wonderful source of inspiration. We collect pictures of men wearing individual pieces that we find beautiful, or men who have put their clothes together in a beautiful way, but always with our central idea in our head. We start with an enormous pile of images, mostly historical, but also some contemporary, and begin the process of disassembling their outfits and rebuilding them in our minds as parts of a contemporary wardrobe. We are driven more by the desire to create pieces of lasting elegance than by producing something that is overtly fashionable in a traditional sense, so it is in the small details of simple styling that we tend to find most inspiration.

What fuels your design ideas?

Claire's view is that research is everything; it stimulates ideas. Claire is a firm believer in constantly having your eyes open to everything around you. We draw inspiration from a huge number of sources; men we see strolling through Mayfair, books on menswear, books on men, old posters, advertisements, our bespoke customers on Savile Row, our clothing archive, museums, cloth stock books (both from our own archive and those of the mills that we use), galleries, architecture, product design, flea markets, antiques (James is an amazing collector of militaria, both objects and images) and anything else that we might stumble upon. We are an English house, but at the heart of what we do is the idea of the inquiring Englishman at large, so we also get our inspiration from our travels. Claire is hugely inspired by Japanese art, fashion and culture; I tend to travel more to Europe and the north-eastern United States. I like the more unusual collections, like the Pitt Rivers Museum in Oxford. You get a tangible sense of the character of one extraordinary Englishman from this most incredible of collections containing everything from million-feather capes to giant keys. Tautz's heritage is sporting and military and there are certain films that resonate strongly with our ideals and help us to keep ourselves consistent. We watch films such as *Lawrence of Arabia* (1962) or *Chariots of Fire* (1981), not just for the costumes but also for the pervading sense of British elegance under even the most testing circumstances.

Does your design process involve photography, drawing or reading?

We use a lot of photography in our research process, but not a great deal during the design phase. Claire's camera is very important to her; she is constantly taking photos of things she likes, whether that be a man in the street, a bicycle, a texture on a pavement, anything, even if at that point she is not sure what we may use it for in the future. We use the camera a little if there is anything tricky that we want to look at on the model and review at the board, and it is obviously vital as we start to dress the completed collection for show. I read as much as I can, mostly biographies and autobiographies, about the men we admire. This forms a substantial part of my research; I like to understand how men I find stylish think about their clothes, and what their contemporaries thought about them and their style. These books are also fantastic sources of images often not seen in other more obvious sources of reference on men's style.

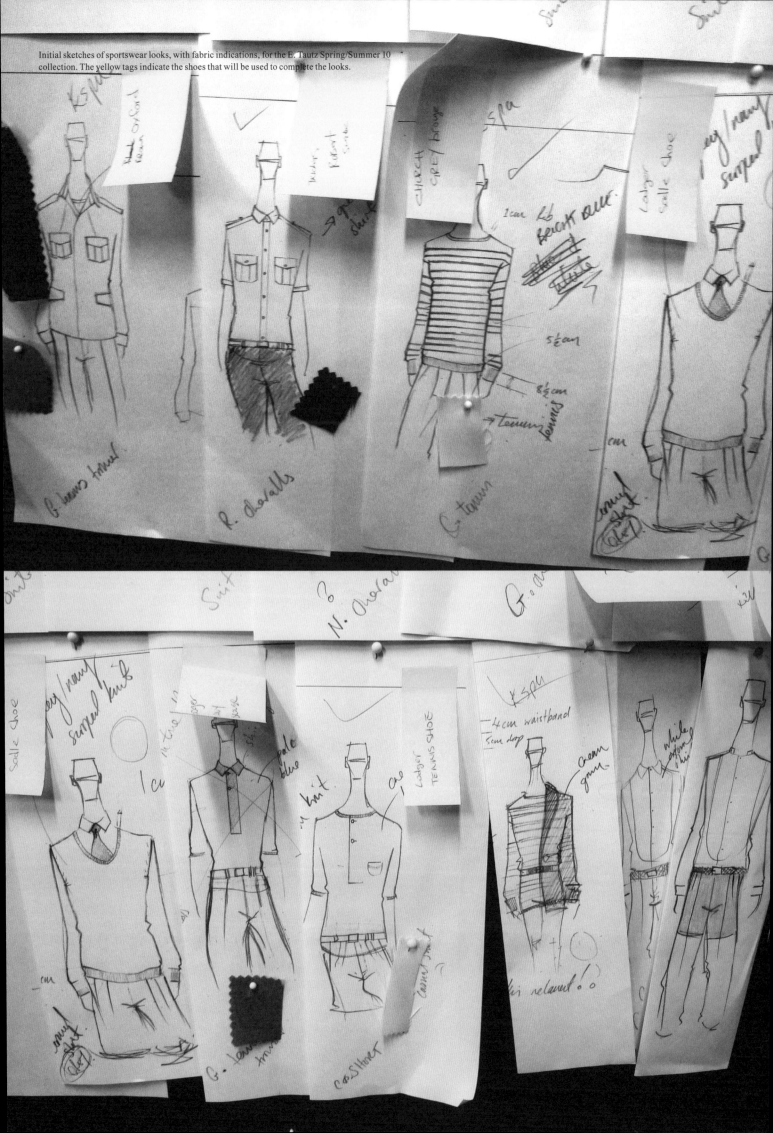

Initial sketches of sportswear looks, with fabric indications, for the E. Tautz Spring/Summer 10 collection. The yellow tags indicate the shoes that will be used to complete the looks.

Mark Eley and Wakako Kishimoto make up Eley Kishimoto. Eley graduated from Brighton Polytechnic in 1990, while Kishimoto, interviewed here, graduated from Central Saint Martins in 1992. Together they launched Eley Kishimoto in 1992, designing prints for such names as Alexander McQueen and Louis Vuitton. In 1995, Eley Kishimoto produced its first collection and has since become recognized for its unique and quirky clothes that use both colour and print.

ELEY KISHIMOTO

Is there a routine to your design process?
I would love to find an easy method, but I think I might get bored if I did.

How important is research in your working process?
Research is involved in many stages of the design development, from random flicking through books on all subjects, with no particular purpose except for personal curiosity, to the need for technical information on a more practical level. I remember, record, collect, write and sketch. I tend to spend a big part of my time drawing for various design purposes.

What is the most enjoyable part of designing for you?
When I sense that all the ideas start to work together.

What are your sources of inspiration?
A mixture of things and whatever draws my attention. It could be a visual attraction, a technical study or even just a feeling.

How would you describe your design process?
It's a journey from my head to the end products; sometimes it's quick and easy, or it could be congested, delayed, detoured, lost or even cancelled. But I often find this journey gives me new openness for ideas.

Is there a specific time of day when you are most creative?
It changes, but I tend to deal with the practical side of creativity during the day and undertake more thinking in the evening.

What fuels your design ideas?
Sensing little sparks in my head makes me go on to the next stage. I can't explain in words what triggers them each time.

What materials are essential to your working methods?
As I still work most of the time in an analogue way, I have many tools and implements that I rely on, from paintbrushes to silk screens. But, if I have to nominate the essentials, it would be the pen and paper nearest to me.

What is the best environment for you to work in?
My workroom in my house, where I can switch between work mode and recreation mode easily.

Do you have a team that is involved in the design process? If so, what do they do?
I wouldn't be doing what I am doing without the support of my team. They help me with design assistance, technical execution, communication and generally organizing my own chaos.

Colour and print are integral to Eley Kishimoto's designs. This fabric collage shows work in progress for print ideas and colour for the Spring/Summer 04 'Butterfly Brigades Nightmare' collection.

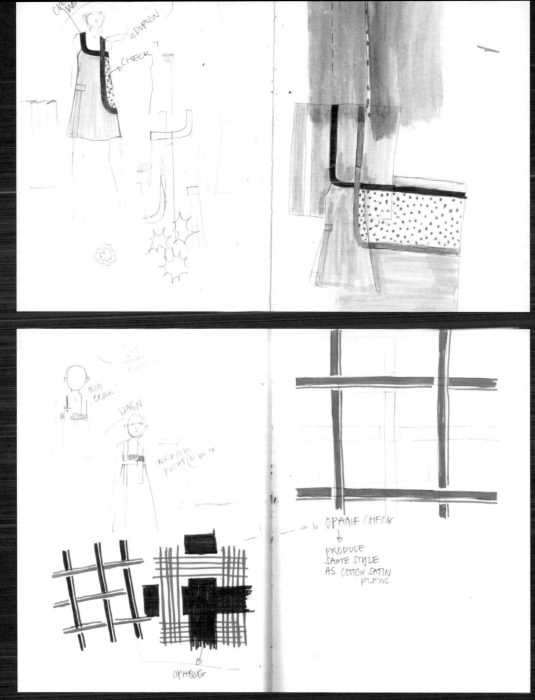

TOP & MIDDLE — Pencil and watercolour studies are used for work in progress print and garment ideas for the Spring/Summer 07 'Back to the Drawing Board' collection. Details for the print ideas are drawn or painted by hand and in media are designed with the garment in mind gives a clear impression of the silhouette and feel of the garments.

BOTTOM — Knitwear sketches from the Autumn/Winter 04/05 collection entitled 'A Hunter and A Potter'. The mark-making technique gives a clear impression of the silhouette and feel of the garments.

OPPOSITE — A dynamic print design entitled 'sweet talk' for the Spring/Summer 06 'Cosmic Dolls on Earth' collection.

OPAQUE CHECK
↓
PRODUCE
SAME STYLE
AS COTTON SATIN
PLAINS.

OPAQUE

BIG
CROWD

UNKIN

→ CROCHET
BUTTONS

SEQUINS

SILVER

KM-44
RAISIN
KM-72
RETICA
KM-92
PLUM

KM-29
ESTRAGON

KM-30
THYM
KM-35
FRAISE
KM-24
EPINARD

KM-10
NERO

KM-74
CHOCOLATA
KM-29
PERSIL
KM-30
TYME

KM-18
MONTARDE
KM-44
RAISIN
KM-71
NUOVA

What fuels your design ideas?
I use everything from film and books to music and photography. I keep folders of things that may not be useful for another couple of years.

Is there a routine to your design process?
My clothes are very textile based, so things always start with the fabric, the print or embroideries.

<u>Do you have a team that is involved in the design process? If so, what do they do?</u>
Cathy Edwards has always styled every show and works with me throughout the whole process. Shona Heath is also involved with the whole ideas part. Although she is traditionally a set designer, she always helps with the print and the showpieces. My husband Neil works on the branding, invites and look books.

How important is research in your working process?
The research process is my favourite part and is massively important for the collections. I love drawing together hundreds of different references and mixing them up so much that you create something completely new. Sometimes a collection starts with the name; for example, 'Lonesome Suzie' was a country song [by The Band] from which came all the references to Americana, widows, black lace, rockabilly culture and beauty pageants.

Do you have sources of inspiration that you <u>always revisit?</u>
Yes, definitely, art nouveau, circus performers and surrealism always creep in.

EMMA COOK

Emma Cook graduated from Central Saint Martins in 1999. She launched her own line during London Fashion Week in 2000, where her Spring/Summer 01 collection established her feminine approach to fashion. Cook's collections are always inspired by a fictional muse named Susan. To create each season's look, Cook imagines her young character travelling through time and the world, thereby informing Cook's use of fabric, print and detailing, which often includes hand-painted and handcrafted touches. Past collections have incorporated whimsical shapes, chintz accents and draped jersey with laser-cut overlays.

Is there a specific time of day when you are most creative?
In the early morning, before the rest of the team arrive, around 8.30 am.

Do you experience a 'eureka moment' when you know a design is working?
I love the last week before a show, when I have finished all of the 'serious' stuff like making dresses that people want to wear and can actually be produced. Then I make a couple of showpieces myself in the studio. These pieces don't need to be produced and we can do something a bit more fantastical. I love this bit.

What is the best environment for you to work in?
I like working in the studio with my friends Cathy Edwards and Shona Heath. We have always worked together and they always play a part in each collection. We come up with the best ideas when we work together and it's really good fun.

A work-in-progress dress being decorated with Swarovski crystals for Emma Cook's 'Lonesome Suzie' Autumn/Winter 08/09 collection. Photography Claire Robertson.

OVERLEAF—
Emma Cook's research wall for her Autumn/Winter 08/09 collection in her East London studio. The inspiration includes fabric, patterns, colour and drawing references.

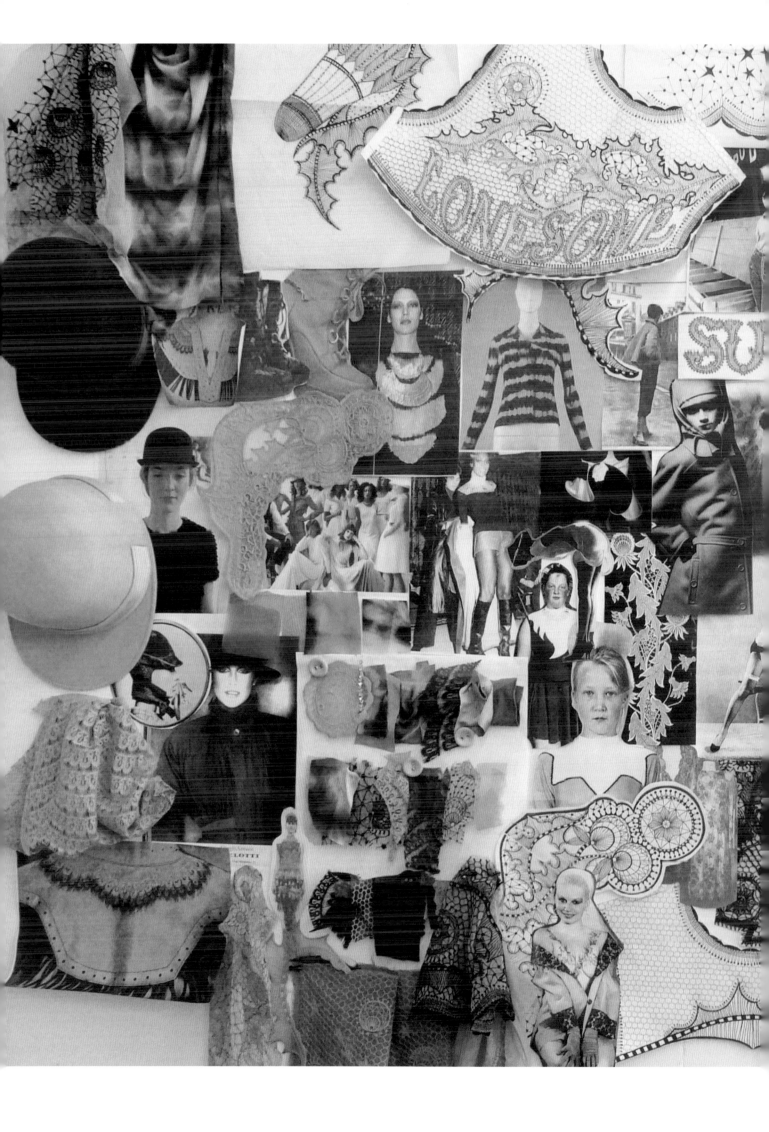

Is there a specific time of day when you are most creative?
The early evening.

What is the most enjoyable part of designing for you?
The most enjoyable part is when everything comes together and you feel confident about the ideas and it suddenly all makes sense together. The difficult part is getting there.

What is the best environment for you to work in?
We always work from our studio. We could not afford a studio for a long time, so we really appreciate our workspace. We have one room from which our team and we work, so it is a very creative environment.

Twin sisters Annette and Daniela Felder attended Central Saint Martins in London. Annette studied Fashion Communication and Promotion, while Daniela graduated in Fashion Design. While at college, the sisters decided to combine their talents and set up the womenswear label Felder • Felder. In 2006, their year of graduation, they were selected by Gen Art to show their collection at New York Fashion Week. Their successful debut pieces defined Felder • Felder's edgy but feminine style.

FELDER • FELDER

How important is research in your working process?
Once we know in which direction we want to go, research plays an important part in our design process. Depending on the inspiration, our research varies a bit every season, but it normally involves watching movies, documentaries, music video clips, going to vintage markets and collecting images that we stick into our sketchbook, and then we start to experiment.

Do you experience a 'eureka moment' when you know a design is working?
Yes, absolutely. You just know when something works, it all falls into place and it all seems very natural and effortless.

What materials are essential to your working methods?
Plain paper and a black pen for sketching. In our sketchbooks, we create collages, so we use photocopies, fabric swatches, pictures, scissors and glue.

How would you describe your design process?
We always find the mood that inspires us, and the icons that fit that particular mood.

NIRVANA ② ② — Tailing
~~Artwork~~ — Fitting
~~Style of~~ DRESSES

burnt black Leather
→ dress COVERED
with
→ SCREWS
and
→ can browns

which are bigger at
Top and grade smaller
towards Hem
silver/gold mix

dress interfaced.

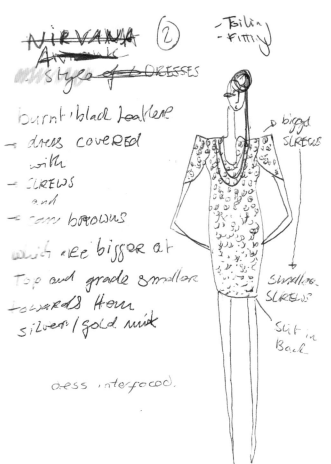

→ bigger SCREWS

→ smaller SCREWS

→ Slit in Back

"Linda"   PC FRAW → PATTERN!
A DRESS

→ Black Leather - NAPPA
→ Black SUEDE OR PATENT
→ Black Chiffon
→ GREY Chiffon (maybe)
→ Black Dowdi for BODICE (maybe)

_____

Experiment!

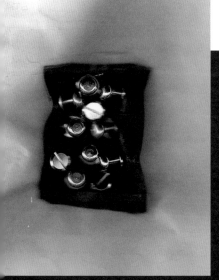

TOP LEFT & BOTTOM LEFT — The drawing shows the design development for the Nirvana dress from the Autumn/Winter 09/10 'Grunge de Luxe' collection. The dress is constructed from leather and embroidered with hundreds of Sam Brownes (buttons and washers), which create a dramatic sparkle effect on the garment.

TOP RIGHT & BOTTOM RIGHT — Design development and details for the Linda dress, the top half of which is made from leather and suede and the skirt is constructed from layers and layers of ruffled silk. The fabric swatch shows how the fabrics are layered together. All artwork is drawn, created and handmade by Annette and Daniela Felder.

How important is research in your working process?

Research can range from finding inspiration in found images and objects to communication with people who surround me. Those people can be artists, writers, musicians or collaborators, all of whom play a vital role in pinning down new areas of research and investigation, be it recommendations in terms of literature, art or even their own, sometimes nearly forgotten, ways of working and crafting. I respect those collaborators and craftsmen who come from a different field but connect with ease with my approach to fashion design. To question, listen to, understand and accept those ways of working and to incorporate their craftsmanship into my designs all leads to important and satisfying results.

FRANK LEDER

German-born Frank Leder studied fashion design at Central Saint Martins in London. During his studies, he also worked on his own collection, which he sold to the boutique Pineal Eye in Soho, London. Leder has been showing his collections in London since 1999, and in 2002 he made his debut at the Paris menswear collections. Leder returned to Berlin in 2002 to celebrate his German identity by creating clothes that are a product of his design environment.

What materials are essential to your working methods?

Ideas do not limit themselves to specific objects: a paper napkin to write on can serve equally as well as one of my black books (which I almost always carry around to hold on to ideas and remarks) as a transmitter of ideas or a reminder.

What fuels your design ideas?

Writers are important in shaping my own design world and include well-known people like Thomas Bernhard, Peter Handke, Siegfried Lenz, Ernst Jünger, Günter Grass and Thomas Mann.

Does your design process involve photography, drawing or reading?

Reading books is important to my design process as books widen my horizons in terms of their descriptions of situations, places and people, which I take as starting points for new collections and designs. Photography also plays a vital role in establishing fields of research and communicating environments and situations, and therefore works as a transmitter of my aesthetic world and background.

Is there a specific time of day when you are most creative?

On a normal day in the office, there are telephone calls, busy assistants and production work to be dealt with. So there is not really time to focus on new ways and pathways. I like to work in the quieter moments of the day – before everybody comes to work or after everybody has left; that's the time of day when new ideas come into focus.

What is the most enjoyable part of designing for you?

The most enjoyable part is the moment when it all comes together as a unit. It is when every piece that has made sense on its own suddenly finds a place in my design universe and connects and speaks its own but also distinctively Frank Leder language.

How would you describe your design process?

It's a naturally evolving path that can lead to unexpected territories. It is enlightening and dark and includes previously unvisited corners and niches of my habitat and design world, but still keeps within the context of my design language and style. I find inspiration by turning back the clock to take a twist on cultural history with a modern approach and goal in mind.

Do you have a team that is involved in the design process?

Designing is a very personal form of bringing together ideas and moments that you have hidden inside yourself for a long time or that you have discovered recently. My name stands inside my garments, therefore this basic work has to be done by myself, nobody else, otherwise I would be untrue to my ideals.

Do you experience a 'eureka moment' when you know a design is working?

For me, 'eureka moments' support but do not lead the way in forming and building new roads and pathways.

Do you have sources of inspiration that you always revisit?

Yes, I undertake a sort of sociocultural study of a Germany of the past to dig out long-forgotten rituals and social contexts. It is a certain romanticized place, which never existed, where a darker place is bubbling under the surface, which you realize only on a second look. There should always be a twist in the tale, though.

Is there a routine to your design process?

Research and design never stop nor can they be limited to certain times. I can be in the middle of producing a new collection when there comes an idea that is so strong and wants to tell a story that I take the idea on board and start immediately to weave it into the context of my work. The important thing is to allow yourself always to be open to new ideas and ways of thinking and perceiving.

TOP — Frank Leder's mood boards are distinctive and communicate his influences for the collection. Inspiration for the Autumn/Winter 08/09 collection entitled 'Hinterland 3: Vagabund' includes maps, photographs, medals and watercolours.
BOTTOM — Image references for the 'Poacher' collection. Autumn/Winter 09/10, which show vintage buttons and historical images of a poacher. Fabrics are also important to Leder at this early stage.

OPPOSITE — Image, fabric, graphic and colour references for Frank Leder's Spring/Summer 09 collection entitled 'Wertarbeit'.

TOP ROW — LEFT — Old photographs and fabric swatches provide inspiration for the 'Back to the Roots' Spring/Summer 06 collection. MIDDLE — Reference material for Leder's Spring/Summer 08 collection entitled 'Hinterland 2: Fleisch', which includes drawings of mechanical objects and old photographs. RIGHT — Frank Leder's studio, showing the designer's distinctive design aesthetic of utilitarian functionalism that also translates to his garments.

BOTTOM ROW — LEFT — Reference images and objects collected for the 'Hinterland 3: Vagabund' Autumn/Winter 08/09 collection. RIGHT — Old books and

32018402866

23

SAMPLE

Производств...
на
ППУзлехпрои...
Пловдив
БДС...

References for knits that are not related to any specific collection, but offer an overview of Leder's knitwear inspiration.

Frank Leder always carries notebooks to document and record his thoughts and inspirations.

Is there a routine to your design process?

It's all in my fingers. Until they start twitching away I only have a very basic outline of what I want to achieve. I am totally at the mercy of the magic in my hands. I personally can't fathom out other designers who sketch and pass on a 2D drawing. For me, it's all about playing around with random things and then seeing how it can be integrated with the body. I like to make miniature sculptures that just happen to have the end purpose to be worn. That's what I love most because of the element of surprise.

How would you describe your design process?

I have a certain vision of something in my head and try to replicate it in 3D, firstly trying the materials I think most suitable. This can be a surface texture or a shape or a silhouette. I start experimenting with prototypes and joining segments together to then fit on to the body. Happy accidents occur and I discover new techniques. I take photos of the pieces pinned to my mannequin to refine and outline the final design. I may then print out that photo and draw over it to make notes. My design process is predominantly about collecting materials and playing with them! However, I do like to treat myself to a week of going to exhibitions. I have to make a break from my commission work and focus on the collection. To make that divide and conscious switch, I try to dedicate a week to unadulterated tourist activities. I regularly miss out on what's going on at museums and galleries as I'm always too busy, so this is my one chance to indulge and catch up. It doesn't directly influence my work but it is a vehicle to getting my creative juices flowing.

What materials are essential to your working methods?

The majority of the time, I mock up tests with paper as it's my most familiar tool. It's cheap and throwaway, but can soon be transformed into a beautiful object. It's great having leftover trial pieces to send in the post as fun mementos to friends. Materials are very specific, so each time I use something different; it dictates its own destiny. You can't force something, and I like the way a design can be governed purely by its fabrication.

Prop maker and accessory designer Fred Butler graduated from the University of Brighton in 2003. After assisting set designer Shona Heath, Butler received commissions to create accessories for fashion magazines such as *ID* and *Dazed & Confused*. She has also made one-off pieces for musicians including Patrick Wolf and Little Boots. In 2008, Butler launched her first official fashion collection of accessories

FRED BUTLER

and her colourful creations have become integral to the new movement in creative accessory design.

What is the most enjoyable part of designing for you?

It's the buzz from producing something you didn't know you had in you. I think that something else channels through my body and I never know what is going to happen. For the very same reason, it can be terrifying. When I'm under a tight deadline, I have to cross my fingers that my subconscious feels like being creative. Otherwise it can be agonizing, which makes the situation worse!

How important is research in your working process?

Research for me is haphazard. I still do prop work, and through those commissions I come across inspiration. Being forced to source unusual materials and make strange objects sparks off ideas for my own line. The two channels of work interlink and coexist in a very fortuitous way in that respect.

Is there a specific time of day when you are most creative?

Do you experience a 'eureka moment' when you know a design is working?

I'm an early bird who likes to catch the worm. I've never identified with artists who thrive on late-night creativity. I'm stagnant, exhausted and usually terror-stricken by the end of the day and least likely to produce anything good. In the early morning when not much is moving, it feels like my very own special time and I have room to relax and create without the relentless attack of emails and phone calls.

Absolutely. It's very adrenalin driven. There is no accounting for when divine inspiration will strike, but when it does, it's very exciting and I don't notice the clock ticking away because it's so much fun. I'm quite geeky and get very involved in detail and the order of how to get to the end result. The process of working out each stage and then identifying what needs to be done next is very satisfying. My main objective is to create surfaces and textures that have never been seen before. This involves layering up different labour-intensive techniques. It's a bit like cooking, I guess. You can have a recipe to follow but it's when you have an instinct to add unexpected elements that the result is refreshingly exquisite.

Do you have sources of inspiration that you always revisit?

I usually pick something that I have made in the past as a starting point. If I kept a little maquette from a previous project that was sidelined, then I'll dig it out for a chance to rediscover it and push the boundaries of what it can do. I'm also very instinctive and just follow feelings that I can't exactly quantify. It's really fascinating to see how your unconscious tallies up with all the other collections each season.

Fred Butler's design process focuses on creating 3D experiments through trial and error as opposed to sketching designs. 'Dodecahedron Collision' artwork from Autumn/Winter 08/09 explores patterns in a log-cabin-inspired patchwork, which experiments with acetate, vinyl, spray paint and origami in iridescent film.

For Autumn/Winter 08/09, Butler explores 3D leather patchwork, which evolved into a 3D dodecahedron ball necklace.

LEFT & BOTTOM LEFT — For Autumn/Winter 09/10, the 'Heliocentric Electric' collection, Butler incorporated disc-shaped experiments in plastic, felt and silver insulation marathon blankets. The designer also made 3D sequins to create optical illusions.

Experiments with quilting for Autumn/Winter 09/10 included hand-painted silks and painting patterns on paper using acrylic paint. References were taken from the patterns for pom-poms.

Does your design process involve photography, drawing or reading?

A lot of my inspiration comes from photography because it is both concrete and sets my imagination free. It's a different process when I use vintage clothes for inspiration. Inspiration can also be drawn from a trip in a city or architecture.

Is there a routine to your design process?

Yes, the steps are always the same but sometimes some of them are slower and harder. More and more, I have to work the fabrics on a mannequin and less in drawings.

Do you have sources of inspiration that you always revisit?

I like to work with sources of inspiration like books and films, but then I choose to forget them and to keep in mind just what I fancied at the beginning. It's more a question of energy and rhythm. For my last few collections, I focused on Bob Fosse and the show he did with Liza Minnelli, Liza with a 'Z' (1972). Also, the energy of Antonio López García's work has been following me for a few collections. And the art-deco style appears every season consciously or unconsciously.

How important is research in your working process?

Fabrics give me lots of inspiration. I see an item of clothing in every fabric I touch and immediately visualize whether it's for me or not. Also, the energy of the previous fashion show presents the mood for the new collection. A magical moment in my fashion show can offer unique and new inspiration for my next collection.

How would you describe your design process?

It is intimate and very hard to convert into drawings at the beginning because there are so many thoughts and inspirations. Drawing makes my process clear and constructing the pattern pieces makes it evident!

GASPARD YURKIEVICH

Paris-born Gaspard Yurkievich studied at the city's fashion school, Studio Berçot, from 1991 to 1993. He worked for Thierry Mugler in 1992, Jean Paul Gaultier in 1993 and assisted Jean Colonna in 1994. Yurkievich went on to found his own label and in 1998 he received funding from the French fashion institution ANDAM and presented his first prêt-à-porter collection in Paris for Autumn/Winter 99/00.

What is the most enjoyable part of designing for you?

I like to see for real what was in my brain. First, it's an intimate, almost secret atmosphere with my team. Then after styling the collection it's super-exposed the day of the show. I like the contrast between the intimate working session and the exciting and stressful exposure on the day of the show or in front of the buyers. The part I like but find harder and harder is making what I have in my mind into drawings that I can share with my team.

How does your research and design work evolve from 2D to 3D?

With my pattern maker – she's been involved in the creation of every collection since I started. Her signature is on all the clothes. Sometimes she starts a question and I interrupt her to finish it…we read each other's minds. We work on 80% of the drawings together, we drape together and we talk about details. Then she starts and things get more precise or we change because the fabric surprises us and inspires us even more.

Do you experience a 'eureka moment' when you know a design is working?

Oh yes, it's magical when all the elements of a collection you've worked on separately come together so evidently and so coherently.

What materials are essential to your working methods?

I give technical drawings to my pattern maker, who is my essential collaborator in building the collection. So I need thin pens to be precise and a computer to be even more precise.

What is the best environment for you to work in?

It's my office at the weekend when nobody is there and the phone does not ring; I can't work in my holiday home or in my flat.

Is there a specific time of day when you are most creative?

Not specifically, but when I exercise I clear my mind and it can be very productive for my creative process.

BACK IMAGE — Pattern pieces are used to cut out fabric before garments are constructed three-dimensionally. As garments are made out of several pieces, each pattern piece is carefully labelled with a reference number.
FRONT IMAGE — Fabric swatches are pinned to a wall in Gaspard Yurkievich's studio and used both as inspiration and reference. June 2009.

i = 23,8m

large

i = 13,2 m

Small

K

K = 55m

brown

(10n)

k = 3,4m

blue

(10n)

Colour is significant to every
aspect of Yurkievich's work.
Watercolour swatches inform
fabric and yarn choice.

Do you experience a 'eureka moment' when you know a design is working?
That sense of excitement when an idea clicks in your mind is so rewarding. What I find so interesting is that it can happen anytime – I think about the collection constantly and it is usually a process of editing down ideas to present an 'essential' mood to represent an ideal woman.

How would you describe your design process?
It's an evolutionary process starting with a collection concept theme that I refer back to in order to keep it focused.

Do you have sources of inspiration that you always revisit?
I never revisit themes or concepts. Usually, each season has a new outlook and a fresh point of view; I find that more inspiring. Often, an object starts a train of thought. I never reference a period in fashion history.

What is the best environment for you to work in?
I draw in my sketchbook anywhere and everywhere, however, I love being in my studio in London, with my dog Bully at my feet and some great music playing.

Does your design process involve photography, drawing or reading?
My design process involves and engages all my senses, so I tend to listen to music (following a theme), take photographs, draw and collect samples and objects (for example, rocks and gems) that can be used in the collection. I have no single way of working, which is what I enjoy about fashion; it is an eclectic mix that stimulates and invokes the seasonal mood.

How does your research and design work evolve from 2D to 3D?
After I have chosen the materials, developed any specific workmanship or technique and designed the piece, I pass the concept on to the pattern cutter and technician to communicate how I would like the garment to be. This tends to be the most crucial part of the process as the team will then interpret your thoughts and make them 3D. This process is most delicate – a designer is only as good as his or her interpreter.

Graeme Black studied fashion at Edinburgh University, graduating in 1989. He worked in London for John Galliano and Zandra Rhodes before moving to Italy in 1993, where he worked as a designer for Les Copains and then as head designer for Giorgio Armani at the Borgonuovo Black Label. In 2001, Black became chief womenswear designer at Ferragamo, and then in 2005 he set up his own label while remaining at the helm of Ferragamo. Potters such as Bernard Leach and Michael Cardew, Italian craftsmanship and the rich textiles

GRAEME BLACK

of Black's native Scotland inspire his collections. Black has carved out a reputation for luxurious and beautiful clothes that communicate his experience of working at the high end of fashion. His collections appeal to a refined customer who requires an elegant approach to clothing.

What is the most enjoyable part of designing for you?
The best part is seeing the idea in your mind translated into a three-dimensional item of clothing. I love seeing the first samples. The worst thing is being able to draw fast enough to get my ideas down before I forget them! That can always be tricky!!

How important is research in your working process?
Research is a fundamental starting point for any collection. I normally have an interest in a subject that I would like to understand further – this can be anything from a sailing boat (S/S09) to precious gems and minerals (A/W09/10). Research inspires me and opens up new ideas that always bring richness and depth to each piece of the collection. For A/W09/10, I visited the Natural History Museum and was awed by the amazing qualities of the gems and rocks on display. This led me to the library to research books, which became the starting point for colours, prints, volume and textures. It was truly illuminating.

What materials are essential to your working methods?
I always draw with a black felt-tip pen and coloured Pantones (usually on a train or plane!). I use a sketchbook for rough ideas, then re-draw and colour in the sequence of the show with indications of fabrics and textures.

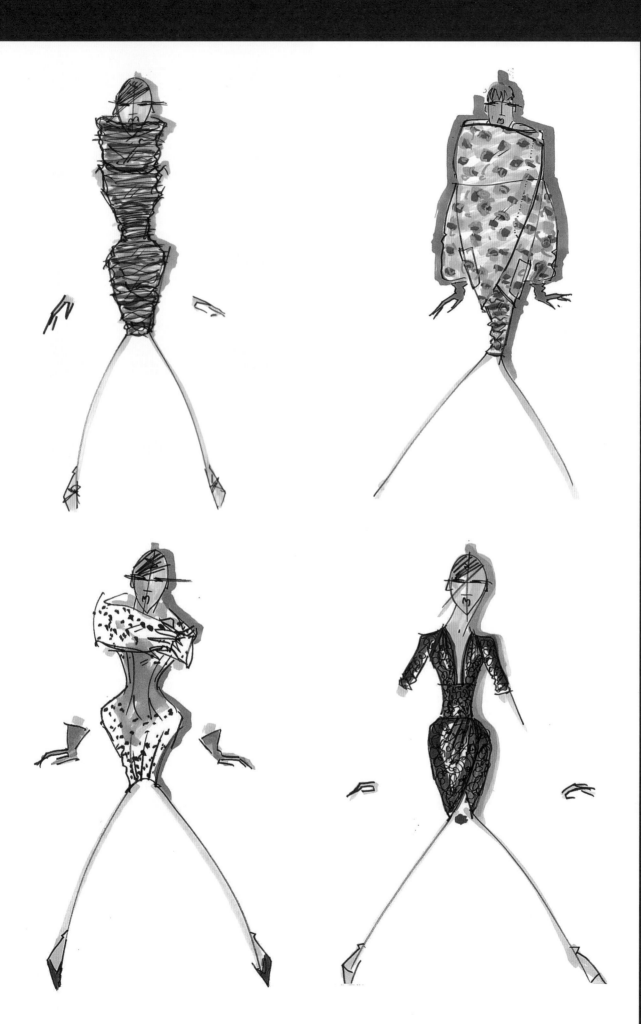

TOP LEFT — A 'Funnel Neck Tulip Jacket' for Autumn/Winter 09/10 is rendered in Pantone pens and gold paint.

TOP RIGHT — 'My design process always starts with honing the chosen concept or mood of the collection and understanding what elements of it can be used to create a truly strong vision for the season,' explains Graeme Black. 'As soon as this is done, ideas for materials arise and evolve and these go on to suggest the shape and structure of each piece.' The designer's illustrations are integral to communicate the mood of his collections. Design for a 'Ribbon Dress' for the Autumn/Winter 09/10 collection.

BOTTOM LEFT — Graeme Black's illustrations are exaggerated in their depiction of the silhouette but they communicate the essence, spirit and attitude of the garments. Shown here is a print tulip skirt bustier dress for Autumn/Winter 09/10.

BOTTOM RIGHT — A tulip drape dress for Autumn/Winter 09/10.

Do you experience a 'eureka moment' when you know a design is working?

The 'eureka moment' comes when I think of something to do in the beginning; the remaining process is a series of ups and downs until the ideas are resolved and realized.

What is the best environment for you to work in?

I think everywhere and jot down ideas on anything to hand, but I can only really focus and immerse myself in the process in my studio, which is my creative cocoon.

HAMISH MORROW

Hamish Morrow was born in South Africa but moved to London to attend Central Saint Martins in 1989. He went on to study menswear at the Royal College of Art. On graduation he was employed by Byblos in Italy and has also worked for Louis Féraud, Fendi and Krizia. In 2000, Morrow returned to London to work on his own line, which he launched during London Fashion Week in February 2001. In 2005, Morrow launched a luxury sportswear collection that used nanotechnology to combine sports and luxury fabrics. With his distinct combination of sport and couture, utility and high fashion, Morrow has established himself in the international fashion world.

What is the most enjoyable part of designing for you?

The best part is dreaming up a collection in the beginning and putting it down on paper. The hardest part is making it real and executing it with perfection.

How does your research and design work evolve from 2D to 3D?

It begins as 3D in my mind, then 2D on paper, 3D on the mannequin as a drape, then 2D as a flat paper pattern, 3D again as a first toile and finally, after corrections and fitting, 3D as a finished garment.

How important is research in your working process?

Research is vital and mostly consists of abstract and non-clothing visuals that are gleaned from anywhere with a few clothing references that are always non-specific. The remainder of the research comes from experimentation and technological research.

How would you describe your design process?

I begin with an abstract concept and several cutting ideas, and from there I evolve the ideas slowly into clothes.

What materials are essential to your working methods?

I always do thousands of thumbnail sketches in black felt tip pen, either in small notebooks or on sheets of cheap copier paper. Then I sketch with an HB pencil, never using colour, and finally I drape with any fabric to hand in the studio.

Is there a specific time of day when you are most creative?

No, inspiration comes when it comes.

Does your design process involve photography, drawing or reading?

My process always starts with ideas, then words in a list form to turn my thought process into black and white. Then follows research, draping, photographing the drapes and finally sketching.

What fuels your design ideas?

Anything and everything, nothing is sacred in the fuelling of creation.

Is there a routine to your design process?

It is always the same order: think, write, research, sketch, material, colour, realize, show.

Do you have a team that is involved in the design process? If so, what do they do?

Often I collaborate with a close friend, Suzanne, who helps me to edit and develop my ideas. I always work with Lisa, my pattern cutter, who turns my thoughts into 3D garments, and of course, my factory in Italy who make the final pieces.

Do you have sources of inspiration that you always revisit?

Yes, contemporary art practice and theory combined with an insatiable appetite for the visual in all forms, mostly film and abstract sculpture.

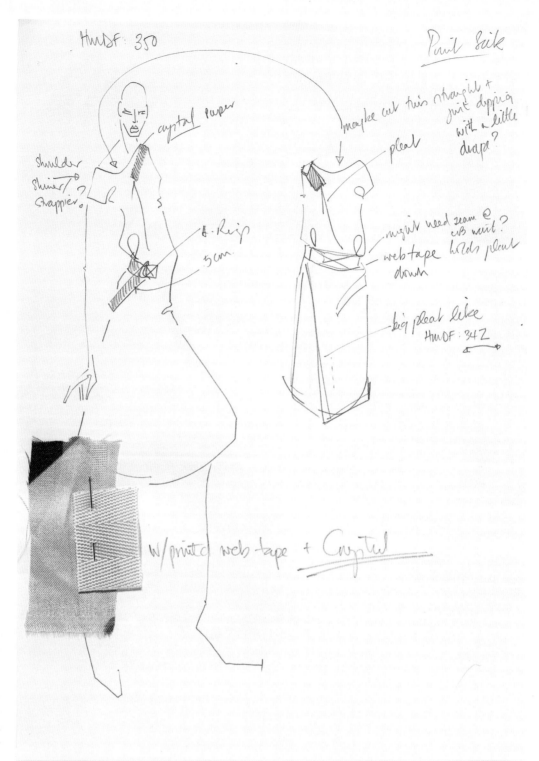

HmDF: 350   Print Silk

crystal paper

shoulder shiner? Grappier.

maybe cut this straight + just dipping with a little drape?

pleat

4-Rip 5cm.

might need seam @ cB waist? web tape holds pleat down

big pleat like HmDF: 342

W/ printed web tape + Crystal

Original sketches by Hamish Morrow showing fabric allocations and construction details for his Spring/Summer 04 collection.

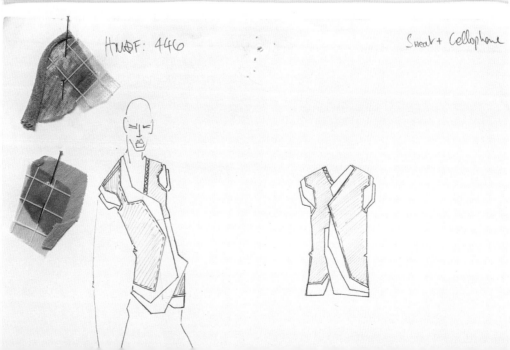

HmDF: 446   Sweat + Cellophane

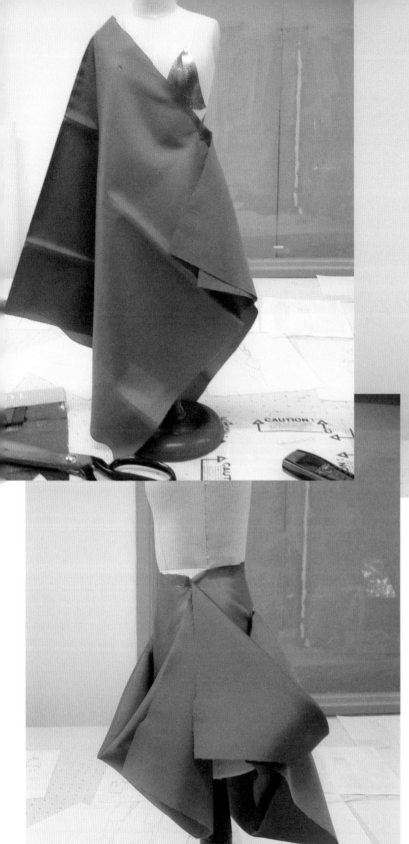

OPPOSITE — Research for the Spring/Summer 04 collection, including hardware, technology, prints, colour, fabric and accessories. Photography by Ela Hawes.

Quarter-scale drape experiments by Morrow for the Spring/Summer 07 collection. These are the first attempts to create the silhouette, and the elimination of first ideas if they are considered visually unsuitable.

Do you have sources of inspiration that you always revisit?

*My science-fiction obsession is always
with me – H. R. Giger, Matthew Barney,
Hieronymus Bosch.*

JEAN-PIERRE BRAGANZA

What is the best environment for you to work in?

**When it comes to designing,
I have to be alone in my studio
with Tool, NIN and Monster
Magnet blasting on the stereo.
And cigarettes.**

Jean-Pierre Braganza was
born in the UK but grew up
in Canada, where he studied
fine art. He moved back to London to study fashion
at Central Saint Martins. After graduation in 2002,
Braganza assisted Roland Mouret before launching
his own collection at London Fashion Week in 2004.
Braganza's aesthetic is dark and is informed by hard
rock, industrial and techno music.

How would you describe
your design process?

*There is never enough time to design, I wish there
was more. In the studio, my time is always sucked
up by emails, production issues, phone calls and all
the tedious stuff that goes with running a business.
When I finally get down to designing it takes a while
to release all of the other bullshit and focus with a
pencil and clean white paper in front of me. I have
to be alone with my music blasting. Then I just let
it come to me.*

How important is research in your working process?

*Research is a part of
everyday life. I envy any
designer who has time to
focus solely on research.
I haven't been able to
do this since college.
You just keep your eyes
and mind open all the
time, and try to expose
yourself to culture
whenever possible.*

**Does your design
process involve
photography,
drawing or reading?**

Always drawing. Sketching on the figure and
erasing and re-drawing until I am happy with
the final look.

How does your research and design work evolve from 2D to 3D?

*My sketches are a very close approximation
to the final result, but ultimately working on
a stand is where the fundamental design is.
That is where I can sculpt and manipulate
the silhouette of the design.*

What materials are
essential to your
working methods?
A mechanical pencil and white A4 paper.

'My design process is quite insular and scattered,' says Braganza. Print plays an important role in his designs and informs the garment shape. The 'Metatrons Cube' print is a fuchsia and black digital print for his Spring/Summer 09 collection.

The 'Purple Eagle' print design for Jean-Pierre Braganza's Autumn/

'Predator' is a grey, pink and silver digital print design that was used in the Spring/Summer 09 collection.

Dynamic and bold illustrations for the Autumn/Winter 04/05 collection communicate the designer's dark approach to fashion. His signature trousers are sharply cut and graphic.

How would you describe your design process?
Curiosity is the most important thing. I think you have to be curious and have the courage of your own convictions. Keep it fresh and keep it exciting, that is the key.

How important is research in your working process?
I start with research and from there I build the muse, the idea, tell a story and develop a character, a look and then a collection.

Do you have a 'eureka moment' when you know a design is working?

When it is fully fashioned, styled, fitted and being worn, then it works

In 2004, *TIME* magazine described John Galliano as 'the most influential fashion designer of his generation'. Born in Gibraltar, Galliano grew up in London and studied fashion at Central Saint Martins. His infamous 1984 degree collection, 'Les Incroyables', was inspired by the French Revolution, and with it Galliano caused his own revolution and his journey into fashion began.

JOHN GALLIANO

Moving to Paris in 1992, Galliano has taken the city by storm, confirming his position at the forefront of fashion and redefining it with every presentation. He spearheaded a renaissance at Dior, and his iconic collections under his own label have become known for breaking the rules. He is one of the most exciting, innovative and romantic designers of our time.

Do you have sources of inspiration that you always revisit?

They are very English. They are a combination of moods, muses and moments. It is high-tech romance with a twist. It could be literature, art or music. I love street culture, uniforms, Savile Row. I love it all. Men or women. Dead or alive. I have many; they are the mood, the colour and the core to creation. Friendships and partnerships are invigorating, inspiring and enriching. The people I meet and work with, the research, the creative process, the show, the clients, I love all of it.

Galliano's imagination, storytelling and research trips are legendary. Each season, he searches the globe, travelling through cultures and continents, referencing literature, the arts and the unexpected to pioneer new ideas. He brings the future, fantasy and romance to life. His shows are one of the most coveted invites in town, with collections taking inspiration from China, Mexico, Russia, Japan and India as well as his homeland. From the Opera Garnier to La Belle Époque, from Bollywood to Las Vegas and from the pearly kings and queens of London to the geishas of the East, Galliano finds beauty in all he sees.

John Galliano's research books are legendary for bringing together his eclectic reference points. On his research trips, the designer draws and photographs his varied and vast inspirations. The books document Galliano's creative design process and include historical research spanning many cultures and periods. Galliano layers the imagery with fabric research and ideas for colour stories. The beautiful books become exciting tools for the design team who reference the inspiration to create narratives for the collections.

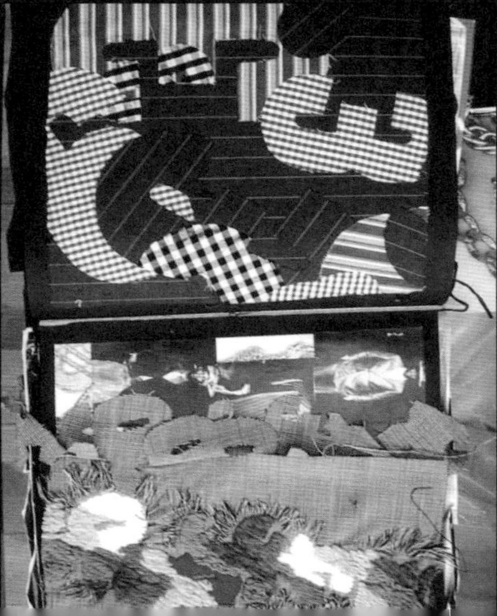

How does your research and design work evolve from 2D to 3D?

The designs are constantly going back and forth between 2D and 3D, often involving minor changes and sometimes changing completely.

Born in Northern Ireland, Jonathan William Anderson originally studied drama at The Actors' Studio in Washington, DC, where he discovered a love of stage costumes. When he returned to

What fuels your design ideas?
Films, books, magazines, archive collections and historical literature.

J. W. ANDERSON

How would you describe your design process?

I start by looking at the mood from the previous season. I then focus on a quote, a phrase or an historical text. I get an idea of a silhouette and use tear-outs and iconic images to create mood boards and to encourage brainstorms. I then work closely with creative director and stylist Toby Grimditch to form the season's looks. We design by look, constantly re-editing and using illustration more than working on the stand.

London, Anderson undertook a degree in menswear at London College of Fashion, graduating in 2007. He made his debut at London Fashion Week in September 2007, showing a menswear collection based around the use of real insects in jewellery. Anderson's collections push the boundaries of British menswear. With his challenging narratives, Anderson is at the forefront of innovation in fashion.

What is the best environment for you to work in?
Late at night, surrounded by my core team, red wine and lots of cigarettes.

Is there a routine to your design process?
We always tend to work in the same way; we have found a way that works well and is enjoyable for everyone, so we stick to it.

What is the most enjoyable part of designing for you?
The most enjoyable part is working with Toby on design and illustrations, and also coming up with fresh new ideas with the whole team late at night. I can honestly say that there isn't a single part of the design process I don't enjoy.

What materials are essential to your working methods?
Winsor & Newton always.

Is there a specific time of day when you are most creative?
Late at night or in the early hours of the morning.

Do you experience a 'eureka moment' when you know a design is working?
We often have 'eureka moments', usually at around four in the morning!

Do you have sources of inspiration that you always revisit?
Each season we always have a 'face' of the season, whether it's a model, actor, artist or musician.

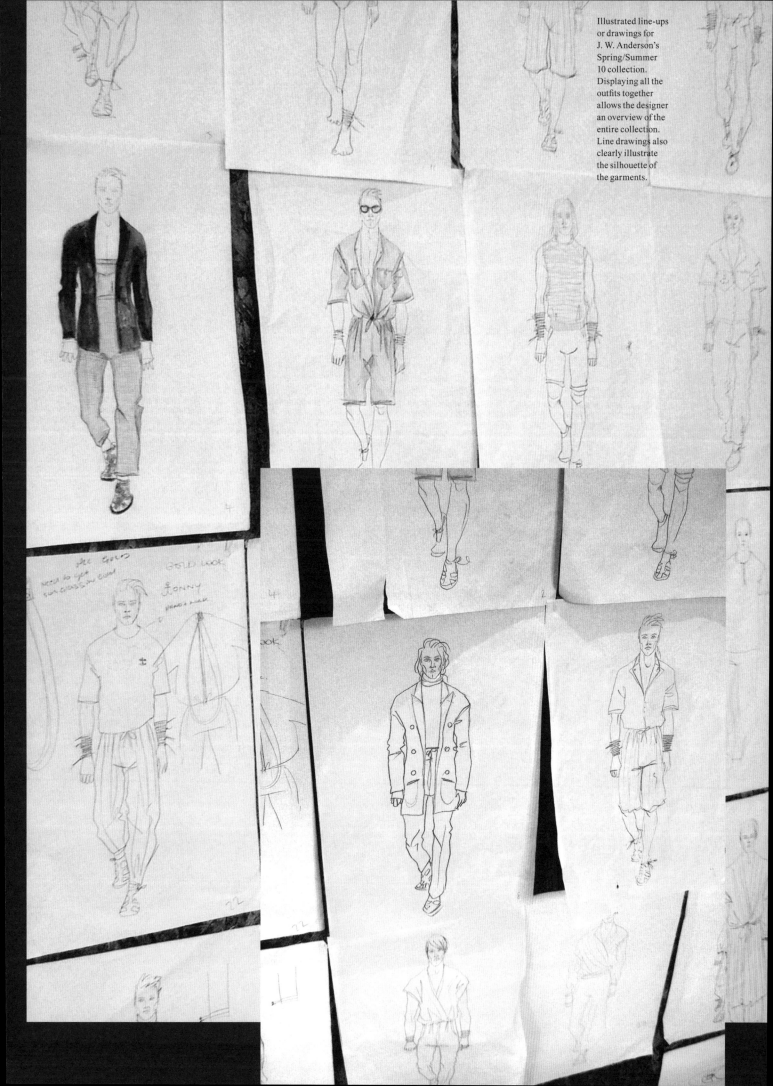

Illustrated line-ups or drawings for J. W. Anderson's Spring/Summer 10 collection. Displaying all the outfits together allows the designer an overview of the entire collection. Line drawings also clearly illustrate the silhouette of the garments.

design development process for J. W. Anderson's Spring/Summer 09 collection.
BOTTOM — Sketches and design ideas for custom-made garments created by
J. W. Anderson for an article in *Dansk* magazine. The pages show how the designer
considers each of his garments should be worn in the appropriate way on the model.

OPPOSITE — A mood board for J. W. Anderson's Spring/Summer 10 collection illustrates the diverse range of influences the designer looks at to inspire his collection. Old fashion photographs, drawings, technical details, flowers and even images of women are pulled together to create a distinct atmosphere and feeling for his collection.

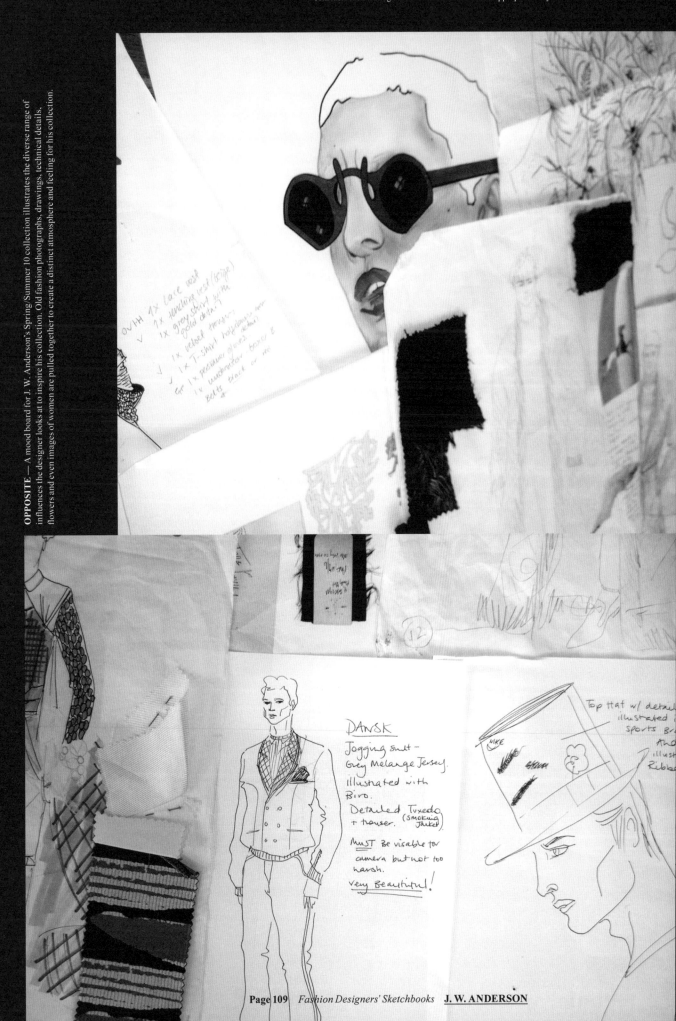

DANSK

Jogging suit –
Grey Melange Jersey.

Illustrated with
Biro.

Detailed Tuxedo
+ trouser. (smoking Jacket).

MUST Be visable for
camera but not too
harsh.
Very Beautiful!

Born in 1933 in Hamburg, Germany, Karl Lagerfeld moved to Paris in 1953. At the age of 22, after coming second in a competition to design a coat sponsored by the International Wool Secretariat, Lagerfeld was awarded a position at Pierre Balmain. In 1963, Chloé invited him to design a pioneering range of luxury ready-to-wear and after three years he began working for Jean Patou.

Lagerfeld set up his own label in early 1984, but he built his name as an independent creator who collaborated with a variety of different fashion labels, including Fendi. However, it was Lagerfeld's appointment to the house of Chanel, one of the strongest brands in fashion, which really put him on the map in 1982. By 1997, *Vogue* had crowned him the 'unparalleled interpreter of the mood of the moment', and he is famed for his versatility and for expertly juggling his roles in various labels, including designing a range for H&M.

KARL LAGERFELD for CHANEL

A recognized illustrator, Lagerfeld states that his fashion drawings are integral to his design process. His favourite materials are a black marker pen and a sketchpad. He conceives his collections through multicoloured drawings on paper and only rarely touches fabric. The loose drawings he produces are often expressive marks that suggest the mood of the collection and are then interpreted by his design team.

With regard to research, Lagerfeld is obsessed with all new things. He buys music magazines, listens to new music and is revered for his capacity to absorb information and specifically for his ability to translate what he consumes into fashion. He says that he has to find out everything there is to know and reads everything. Lagerfeld's determination to stay current and modern requires a certain ruthlessness and lack of sentimentality. He periodically rids himself of art, objects and places that, previously, had been sources of inspiration. Lagerfeld is one of the great designers of contemporary fashion, and his personality as well as his creativity will ensure his place in fashion history.

OPPOSITE MIDDLE — This sewing form was made fully in Chanel workshops before the studio fitting with Karl Lagerfeld. Photo © Stéphane Gaugère.

THIS PAGE — The sketch given to the embroiderers by Karl Lagerfeld will need to be interpreted in the context of the whole collection. The sketch shown here is from the Paris/Moscow 2009 Collection — an ivory organza dress with a sequinned, coloured hem and a top embroidered with white glazed shells, tubes, pearls, golden strips and ivory sequins. One hundred and fifty hours of embroidery were required to create this garment. Photo © Vincent Lappartient to create this garment. Photo © Vincent Lappartient in the Lesage workshops were required to create this garment. Photo © Vincent Lappartient.

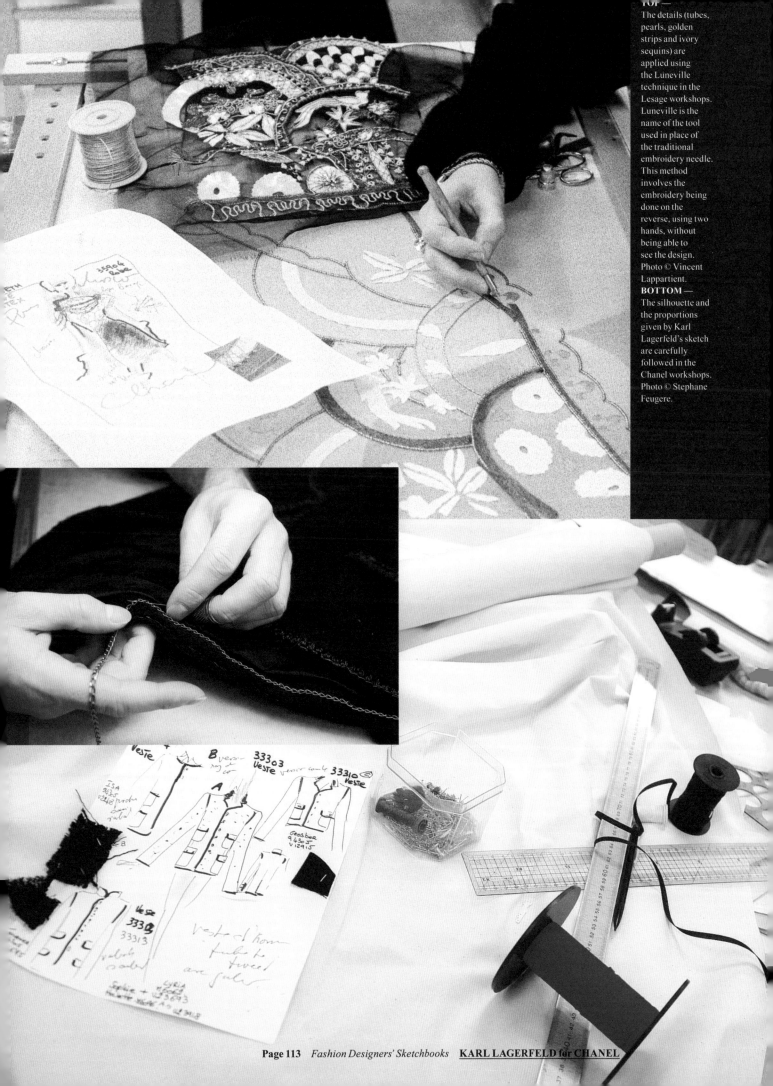

TOP —
The details (tubes, pearls, golden strips and ivory sequins) are applied using the Luneville technique in the Lesage workshops. Luneville is the name of the tool used in place of the traditional embroidery needle. This method involves the embroidery being done on the reverse, using two hands, without being able to see the design. Photo © Vincent Lappartient.
BOTTOM —
The silhouette and the proportions given by Karl Lagerfeld's sketch are carefully followed in the Chanel workshops. Photo © Stephane Feugere.

Graduating from Central Saint Martins in 1988, Kinder Aggugini went on to work on London's Savile Row. He then worked for John Galliano, Vivienne

KINDER AGGUGINI

Westwood and Paul Smith, and later Calvin Klein, Versace and Costume National. Aggugini launched his first collection in 2009. He offers an effortlessly avant-garde wardrobe, undeniably chic with a dark edge. His prevailing inspiration is the fictitious marriage of Coco Chanel to Sid Vicious, with the notion that Coco was more hardcore than Sid; her refined sensibility would have prevailed over rock and roll, but their union would have maintained a certain edge. With intensive research into fabrics, an often obscure approach to detail, a Savile Row-trained eye and a blend of traditional techniques and references with scientifically mastered treatments, Kinder Aggugini proves to be a true modern craftsman.

What is the best environment for you to work in?
Any place is good, but I need tranquillity in my mind. Generally, my home is the best place for me to work.

What fuels your design ideas?
I think of people, real existing people. That way I can think of an outfit as worn by someone and can imagine what fabric, colour, shape and functionality it must have.

How would you describe your design process?
It generally starts with a mood. I begin thinking of something that moves my soul and then I create a story about this feeling, and from it I derive inspiration for a collection. Once I have a mood, I start by creating fabrics and prints, then I develop silhouettes and finally I put the two together. I have something that I can only describe as visual dyslexia, where I often look at something but my mind perceives something else. Interestingly, that vision is more exciting than the reality. I use these images either for something I'm working on or I store them in my visual bank.

Does your design process involve photography, drawing or reading?
Certainly photography. I collect old photos from 1900 to 1930. I spend a little time drawing and a bit reading. Often when I read a book, there might be a description of a person that makes me think of a look and therefore specific garments.

Is there a specific time of day when you are most creative?
Generally at night.

Do you have sources of inspiration that you always revisit?
Emotions are the creative propeller for my designs. I have an immense visual library logged in my brain and draw from that to start the first ideas. Once I get going, I find more and more steam just by looking at the people who surround me.

What materials are essential to your working methods?
I'm very tactile, so primarily I need the cloth from which I'm going to develop a design.

How important is research in your working process?
I spend a great deal of time researching shapes and details. Primarily I like searching for existing garments, but when I can't find what I want I go through old photos, books or images on the Internet.

What is the most enjoyable part of designing for you?
I find it all enjoyable; I love this job. Ever since I can remember I always wanted to be a designer. However, I always find it daunting. Every time I start a new collection I have a great fear that it might not be as good as the last one. It isn't until I do the show fittings that I get an idea of how it all went. The most difficult part is getting the prototypes to become perfect samples.

Do you experience a 'eureka moment' when you know a design is working?
At times I do. It's that moment when I see a garment that I wasn't sure how to construct and it looks exactly like what I had in mind. All of a sudden it is like someone has switched on the lights, and a piece of design has become so clear that I know exactly how it is going to work.

Kinder Aggugini's sketchbooks show research and design development ideas. The top book shows an appointment list for fabric trade show Première Vision, with details of which cloths Aggugini found interesting for his Spring/Summer 09 collection.

SECOND ROW FROM TOP, LEFT — A study for a Highlander jacket in red cashmere for Autumn/Winter 09/10 and a drawing for a velvet devoré dress for the same season.

SECOND ROW FROM TOP, RIGHT — On the left is a print placement for a folded sleeve dress for Spring/Summer 09, and on the right page is an idea for a cadet jacket to be worn with the dress.

THIRD ROW FROM TOP, LEFT — On the left, information about the cloth, details and finishing for a jacket. On the right page, the original reference for the cadet jacket showing details of stitching.

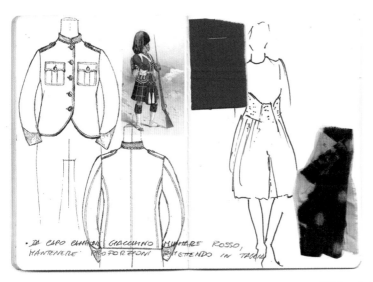

· DA CAPO CAMPINA GIACCHINO MILITARE ROSSO, MANTENERE PROPORZIONI RISTRINGENDO IN TAGLIA

THIRD ROW FROM TOP, RIGHT — A drawing shows jacket construction, cut and details for Autumn/Winter 09/10.

BOTTOM ROW, LEFT — Left page is a study for a top or dress with a chiffon round-the-neck tie and bow for Autumn/Winter 09/10. On the right page is a drawing of a dress with fabric placement for Autumn/Winter 09/10.

BOTTOM ROW, RIGHT — Initial concept for Aggugini's menswear collection for Autumn/Winter 07/08.

WJ01
CADET JACKET
LYRIA Art ZAFATA
salt finish.

ASK RICCARDO
TO FINISH LINEN
WITH SALT
WASH AND
DRY IN TALCUM

COLLAR AND
FACING
IN BLACK
TWEED
(LINTON)

PINTO
AVI ALMANK
PRINT
FIORI ROSSI
(CUT
BLACK
PART
ALSO
FOR SIZES)

23cm

Harris Tweed + Velvet

What is the best environment for you to work in?
Strangely my mind always seems to race when I'm sitting on a train and just looking out of the window. Also, I love being in the office at the weekend when there's nobody around.

Do you have sources of inspiration that you always revisit?
Yes, people. My single most important source of inspiration is always people. I could sit for hours looking at how people move, how they live in their clothes, how their clothes move around them. I look in the relationship between body and garment, the covering and uncovering, the gestures that go with wearing clothes.

What materials are essential to your working methods?
Just a crayon.

How would you describe your design process?
I continuously note or scribble down ideas or details or just things that catch my eye, without deciding whether any of it is worth keeping or using. Whenever I start a new collection, I go through those 'visual diaries' and decide what I would like to do. In a way, my design process is like a soap opera, with a cliffhanger every six months.

What is the most enjoyable part of designing for you?
The most enjoyable part is always the beginning, when everything still seems possible. Every new collection is like a new beginning.

LUTZ

German Lutz Hüller spent three years working for Martin Margiela after completing his fashion design studies at London's Central Saint Martins. He took a creative break in 1999 to investigate his interest in clothing. His first collection was shown in Paris in February 2000 and established Hüller's philosophy of 'decontextualization', which is concerned with taking things out of context, mixing and matching styles and genres and cutting and pasting elements together.

Do you have a team that is involved in the design process? If so, what do they do?
It is important to have a female opinion, and having somebody with a fresh mind come and look at things after a little while always puts things into perspective.

Do you experience a 'eureka moment' when you know a design is working?
Yes, and it's the best moment and really worth the hassle. Although, me having a 'eureka moment' does not necessarily mean that the rest of the studio agrees.

How important is research in your working process?
The research becomes very focused once I have decided on a theme or idea, and can vary from watching a movie again and again to looking at a certain person or taking photos of moving fabric or just listening to the same record obsessively.

Is there a specific time of day when you are most creative?
Yes, during caffeine-fuelled early morning bouts of energy and late at night when everything slows down.

Images for Lutz's Autumn/Winter 03/04 collection. The photographs are working experiments to decide how to style the garments together for the designer's fashion show.

DEFILE TAILLE HAUTE IDRAPÈS

MINI DRAPÉ
→ A ESSYER
Maille Vernis
en dessous

+ Maille Vernis
En dessous

ESSAYER GANTS
MOHAIR

T SHIRT
TRANSPA

DA DRAPEGGIARE
CON SCIARPA
IN MEZZO.

DEFILE FRANGES

+ CAPUCHÉ

FRANGES
NOIRES

FRANGES
ROUGES.

TOUT
NOIRE
FRANGES
ROUGES.

PANTALOURÉ:
TISSU DIFF.

GIACCA LANA NERA
+ CAPUCCIO

FRANGE ROSSE!

SOTTO
MAGLIA?

Do you have sources of inspiration that you always revisit?

A typical elegance is the catchword of the collection and is embroidered on Marchand Drapier labels. I always try to revisit the codes of male elegance. The collection is the ideal wardrobe for the modern man. The tailoring of the twentieth century is one of the sources of inspiration that I revisit season after season.

Designer Benoît Carpentier comes from a family of tailors that goes back five generations. His brand, Marchand Drapier, aims to revive the tailoring spirit of the twentieth century with a contemporary edge. Carpentier offers men beautiful fabrics and perfect cuts, but always includes a subtle humour in his designs that makes the clothing unique and desirable.

MARCHAND DRAPIER

What fuels your design ideas?

Books feed my daydreams. I love historical fiction, which helps me to escape and gives free rein to my imagination. Photographs and strong images from art books deeply inspire me. It is not unusual for me to copy some of those pictures and stick them in my collection books so they follow me through the entire collection. I use fashion magazines in two ways. Sometimes, they act as a deterrent: if I see a particular item or detail several times I am put off and am forced to move on to something else. On the other hand, press reports can comfort me in my ideas and open up new horizons. Strolls in antique shops and flea markets are very enriching. The wealth of the past inspires me, be it the mother-of-pearl inlays in the black wood of a Napoleon III cabinet or the subtle colour combination of a 1950s Vallauris ceramic. Again, I take photos that I pin in my collection books. All through the process, I draw details and write down my ideas on paper. I quickly scribble ideas next to samples of fabric stapled in my notebooks.

Is there a specific time of day when you are most creative?

My creativity is on the boil all day and night. Ideas come and go, hence the importance of having my design books nearby to write down these thoughts.

How would you describe your design process?

It all starts with a desire, a recurrent obsessive desire. It's a craving for a period or a place. I then start writing and filling up my notebook with words, ideas and phrases. These ideas lead to a story and the story leads to new ideas.

What materials are essential to your working methods?

My leather-bound Hermès drawing books go everywhere with me. Since my wife Emille bought me the first book when we started the Marchand Drapier adventure, I cannot design a collection without them. It took me six months to write my first words and I was paralyzed just looking at the blank pages of the book. Following a delayed plane, I found myself stuck in Brussels airport for a few hours and finally started writing. In one go, I wrote the whole story of Marchand Drapier, from the meaning of the name to the vision of the future boutiques. I sketched the labels there and the book now acts as my 'bible', which I consult before and during each collection.

What is the best environment for you to work in?

I am a nomadic person and travel a lot; airports with their multitude of travellers passing each other inspire me enormously. I also like to work late at night in the office in my home, which allows me to be near my family.

How important is research in your working process?

Research is about devouring details of the period and the place to enrich my story. These discoveries lead to new research and a multitude of possible paths (where one musn't get lost). From these discoveries, I try to transform and adapt the male wardrobe. First of all, I search for raw materials. Fabrics are the foundations of my creative process. Thanks to my roots and my fifteen-year career as a textile agent, I have a very close relationship with fabric. The creation process is launched at Première Vision in Paris. The materials and accessories I find there guide me and comfort me in my original ideas. They help me to build up the collection.

Inspirational and atmospheric photographs help to create the mood and feeling of the collections. The pictures were taken at Hotel Raffael in Paris and communicate character, charm and history, all of which are integral to the brand. Photography by Julien Magre.

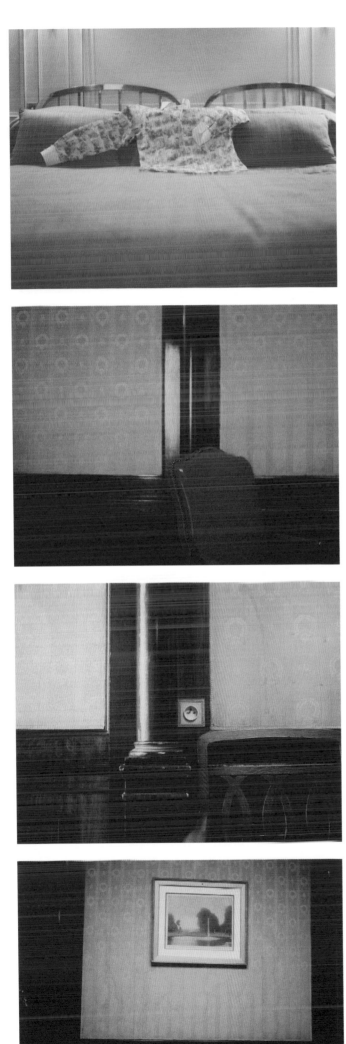

GORi

60709

col 106.

PAGE 121 — Research gathered together for the Autumn/Winter 07/08 collection, including fabrics, accessories and initial design drawings and sketches.

Page 123 *Fashion Designers' Sketchbooks* **MARCHAND DRAPIER**

I always used to draw my ideas for clothes. The drawings were more about creating a mood or a feeling rather than being a specific technical drawing. My drawings are very loose and are more about a style than an exact representation of a garment.

Margaret Howell studied Fine Art at Goldsmiths in London, graduating in 1969. Well-made, quality products are fundamental to Howell's design approach, and in 1970 she starting designing honest, skilfully constructed clothing. Opening her first menswear shop in 1977 on South Molton Street in London, Howell now has three stores in the UK and 56 in Japan.

'I am often inspired by

MARGARET HOWELL

the method by which something is made. I find men's clothing more interesting than women's in its structure, feel and functionality,' explains Howell, who believes that her customers value the fabric, construction, fit and comfort of her designs. Howell has a sensible approach to design. 'Good design has to work. Clothes have to work for people just as a chair has to be comfortable to sit in.' Successful styles from each season are advanced with slight variations in the next collection. 'I like to try and get the best design I can in the first place, and if it works, we may try a different fabric or slightly change the details,' she states.

Often, Howell's customers return and request the same garment that they bought in previous seasons, aligning themselves to the low-key aesthetic. 'They are not interested in wearing their brand on a shirt or on their belts,' she says. 'They associate with what our brand stands for, which is quality and lasting design.' Howell is committed to British manufacturing, traditional production techniques and quality fabrics. Her clothes are simple and understated. With a personal interest in architecture and product design, Howell is a keen supporter of British modernist design.

How important is research in your working process?
For me, it is ongoing. I am always looking at exhibitions, books, magazines, old outfitters, hardware shops, workwear and uniforms.

How would you describe your design process?
It can vary. Sometimes, inspiration strikes and an idea just comes. Sometimes, an image or a photograph is inspiring, and occasionally someone on the street can inform my work. And, fabric plays such an intrinsic part for me that the process usually starts with a response to fabric and an idea of what to use it for. Sometimes, I start from a manufacturing process and that dictates the design.

Margaret Howell's original pen and ink drawings for her first shirt designs in the early 1970s. A collarless shirt with contrast collar band is shown at the top, while a welt-pocket shirt is seen bottom left and an irregular-pocket shirt bottom right.

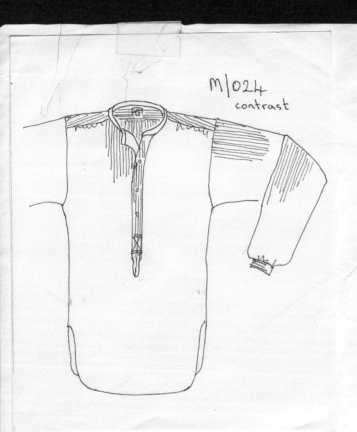

m/024
contrast

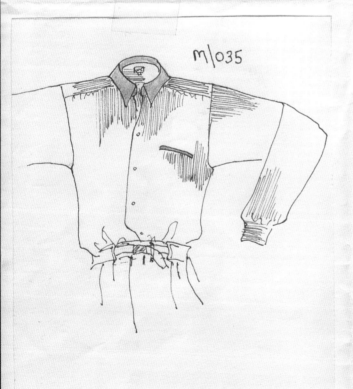

m/035

m/052

LEFT — Margaret Howell's design assistant's pencil line drawings for the women's Spring/Summer 2000 collection.
RIGHT — Wool tailoring and tweed fabric selection, c. 1994. Fabric choice defines Howell's collections as high-quality material is core to the brand's aesthetic.

TOP LEFT — Pencil drawing of the 'school coat' concept for the women's Autumn/Winter 90/91 collection. Howell's drawings communicate not just the design of the garment but also the mood and spirit of the collection.

TOP RIGHT — Pencil drawing for the 'one-button shirt' in white cotton with one large mother-of-pearl button in the Spring/Summer 98 collection.

BOTTOM LEFT — Pencil drawing for the 'army trouser' concept for the men's Autumn/Winter 95/96 collection.

BOTTOM RIGHT — Pencil drawing for a shirt, c. 1999, but originally designed in 1970.

full swagger
raincoat.
3/4 length.
fly front?
good warm belt.

Margaret Howell, 89

A pencil mood drawing by Margaret Howell in 1989 for a 'swagger' raincoat.

Natural raw-silk pyjama bottoms using blue selvedge are part of the women's Spring/Summer 2000 collection.

Polaroids are used for model casting for the Autumn/Winter 09/10 show during London Fashion Week in 2009.

MARK FAST

Canadian knitwear designer Mark Fast studied both a BA and an MA at Central Saint Martins, graduating in 2008. Creating knits by hand or on a domestic knitting machine, Fast blends Lycra with yarn to create volume and sculptural shapes over the body.

How important is research in your working process?

I have to create a story. I make a film-like storyboard to illustrate it and thrive off the emotion of the story to inspire the clothes. Different characters get different looks that give them their own personal attitude.

What is the most enjoyable part of designing for you?

I love seeing the piece on a woman and seeing her enjoy having it on. There are always a lot of difficulties and things I don't like, but the good ultimately outweighs the bad.

What materials are essential to your working methods?
Elastic yarn mostly.

Is there a specific time of day when you are most creative?
Two in the morning when there are no distractions, just peace.

What is the best environment for you to work in?
My favourite place is my studio. It's a great atmosphere. It's a very grimy area, but there is a lovely canal I walk along near the graffiti-covered warehouses.

Do you experience a 'eureka moment' when you know a design is working?
I love those moments, yes.

How would you describe your design process?
It's quite organic. It's very abstract expressionist.

Does your design process involve photography, drawing or reading?
I do quite a lot of sketching, but most of it occurs on the knitting machine.

What fuels your design ideas?
I look for amazing books with fantastic, severe images in them.

Do you have sources of inspiration that you always revisit?
It all comes back to the female body.

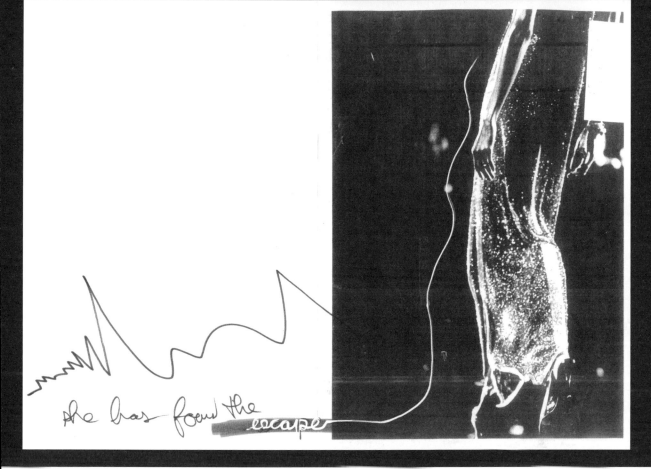

the has found the escape

her kingdom is not hers anymore

Egyptian-inspired colour references for
Mark Fast's Spring/Summer 10 collection.

Initial drawings showing how Swarovski pearls are integrated with knitwear for the Spring/Summer 10 collection.

'A collage of the objects that the queen takes with her as she escapes. This is one of her prized possessions and it is a reference for the textures used in the show for Spring/Summer 10.'

An illustration for the Spring/Summer 10 collection. 'I wanted to create a shimmering, mystic Egyptian mood by linking crystals into my knitwear,' explains Fast.

CRYSTAL
PEARL
BRACELET

AND

SWOOPING
CRYSTAL
PEARL
HARNESS

CRYSTAL
PEARLS
LINKED

*Do you have sources
of inspiration that
you always revisit?*

I have always been extremely passionate about travelling, and I like to take time out to relax and recharge my batteries for the season ahead. This doesn't mean I have to go somewhere quiet, on the contrary I find staying somewhere that has a lively atmosphere and a real buzz about the area invigorating. I spend most of the days looking round local markets for my next collection's research; a small trinket box I bought on one such occasion had intricate mother-of-pearl inlays that inspired a print. I am a prolific photo-taker, and often when looking back over the images I have taken in the past, I notice a small interesting detail that turns out to be a major theme in my next collection. The destinations I am drawn to tend to be hot, exotic and colourful and have long inspired the vibrant colour palette that I am known for.

Do you experience a 'eureka moment' when you know a design is working?
There is most definitely an extremely exciting, albeit slightly apprehensive, moment when all the calico toiles appear in their correct cut, digital prints jump off the screen on to flowing fabric, beading placements are finalized and the ideas and themes considered months earlier suddenly come to fruition. All these different aspects do not come together until a very late stage, sometimes only days before presenting the collection on the runway. At this point, editing is the most important factor and works to condense all the ideas and to make sure that the story is clear and all components are complementing each other.

For sketching, I prefer to use a fine pencil for greater definition. However, I am equally happy to sketch with a simple biro in my Smythson notebook if I am out and about.

What materials are essential to your working methods?

What is the most enjoyable part of designing for you?
An important part of the brand DNA has always been an element of juxtaposition, such as nature and the synthetic, vintage and modern. My most enjoyable time during the process is spent finding fresh ways of presenting this clash to the best effect. It is an experimental period when we discuss many different combinations of colour, fabrics, trimmings, embellishments, silhouettes and production techniques.

MATTHEW WILLIAMSON

Is there a routine to your design process?
The process always begins with a visit to the international fabric fairs and also to the mills that produce our cloth to find out about new developments or techniques that could be used. Then we gather together any significant inspiration and compile a mood board to visually represent the silhouette, colour palette or tone of the collection. At this point, development can vary. Sometimes the chosen fabrics dictate a certain silhouette and so I would begin to sketch out shapes to explore the proportions, and print and beading would then be developed to complement this. But, equally, the beading could be the main focus for the collection and used to communicate the central theme, so placement and sourcing would then take precedence and lead the progression of the cut. The whole process is very organic and there is no set way in which we work, instead it can be defined as an evolving course.

With a BA in Fashion Design and Printed Textiles, Matthew Williamson graduated from Central Saint Martins in 1994. He founded his own label in 1997 and his debut collection of bright and intricately detailed dresses, entitled 'Electric Angels', defined and set the pace for the highly successful Matthew Williamson aesthetic. In 2002, Williamson showed for the first time at New York Fashion Week, and in 2005 he took over as creative director at the Italian house Emilio Pucci, while continuing at the design helm of his own company. Williamson is renowned for bringing a sense of colour to fashion and continues to explore colour as the driving force behind a collection.

Does your design process involve photography, drawing or reading?

Often the research I undertake while travelling results in us absorbing elements of an area's local culture. This leads us to investigate the techniques they use to achieve a given effect, and how we may translate this into a modern collection. For example, we took the Asian- and African-rooted tie-dye process, which traditionally uses natural dyes on cotton, but applied it in vivid neon to a luxurious silk. Elsewhere, we will perhaps take the essence of an indigenous artwork or movement to inspire beadwork or embellishment, always ensuring we have undertaken sufficient research to reference this faithfully.

How would you describe your design process?
My personal method is very alchemic, constantly changing from the early stages to the final collection. I begin with a nugget of inspiration, and this small idea can be developed to become the whole theme of the show. A good example of this is a vintage carpet bag I found a few years ago, which inspired the 2007 winter collection's theme and the floral motif was reinterpreted in a graphic print.

A girl on a holiday inspired Matthew Williamson's Spring/Summer 09 collection. The design drawing illustrates block-colour tailoring and an Amboise print dress.

How important is research in your working process?

I like to study antique and vintage clothes. My favourite thing is to see something that is old. I learn and discover a lot from vintage clothes because they tell me the history and culture of where they are from.

What are your sources of inspiration?

Nothing especially, but my memory and illusions of daily life. Creating new ideas and forms of expression.

Born in Japan, Mihara Yasuhiro graduated in textile design from the Tama Art University in Tokyo in 1997. Yasuhiro taught himself the traditional methods of shoemaking, and in 1996, while still at college, he launched the shoe label Archi Doom, which evolved into the Mihara Yasuhiro label in 1997. In 2000, Yasuhiro began a collaboration with PUMA to create the PUMA by Mihara Yasuhiro Collection. With a design philosophy to break through stereotypical boundaries with witty, eclectic and beautiful clothes, Yasuhiro launched his first menswear collection in 2004.

Is there a specific time of day when you are most creative?
I don't have a specific time for creation.

Does your design process involve photography, drawing or reading?

I'm afraid to use images because they can give too strong an effect. Of course, drawing is important to express the image and idea in my mind. When the image in my mind appears on paper, I have no feeling. Developing ideas from a sentence in a book is essential and is like alcohol. I want to feel and be intoxicated by a good sentence.

Is there a routine to your design process?
It is not always the same. It depends on the situation. I believe that representation has to be pure.

What is the best environment for you to work in?
My desk at the office (a big black steel desk!).

What fuels your design ideas?
Fetishism, humour and a pinch of opposing ideas.

Do you have a team that is involved in the design process? If so, what do they do?
All my assistants are excellent and they understand my ideas and designs. They spend a lot of time developing material, special processing techniques and specific patterns.

How would you describe your design process?
I always start an idea by sketching and writing a sentence. I build up the design by following the idea as closely as possible.

How does your research and design work evolve from 2D to 3D?
I am very interested in the fourth dimension. What is the fourth dimension? My purpose is to research and design to create a gap between vision and sense.

What materials are essential to your working methods?
Several types of Post-it notes and a sharp pencil.

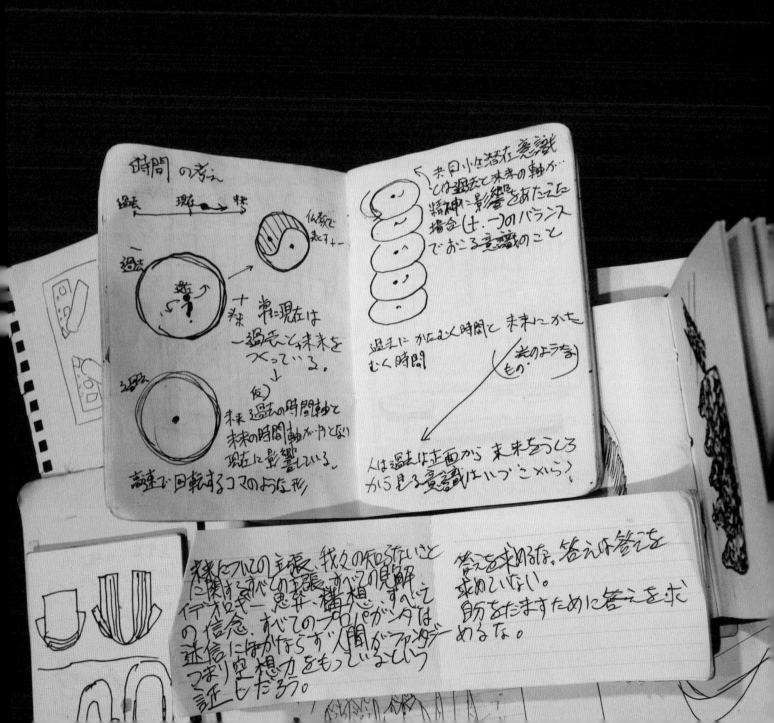

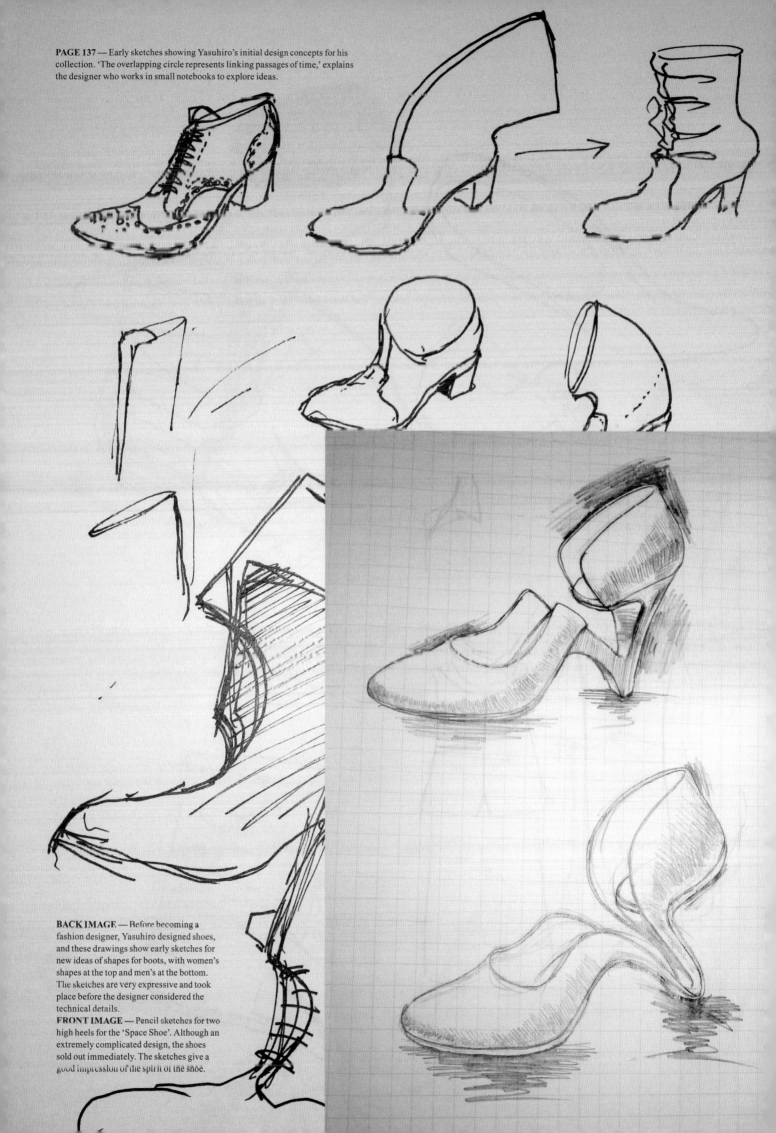

PAGE 137 — Early sketches showing Yasuhiro's initial design concepts for his collection. 'The overlapping circle represents linking passages of time,' explains the designer who works in small notebooks to explore ideas.

BACK IMAGE — Before becoming a fashion designer, Yasuhiro designed shoes, and these drawings show early sketches for new ideas of shapes for boots, with women's shapes at the top and men's at the bottom. The sketches are very expressive and took place before the designer considered the technical details.

FRONT IMAGE — Pencil sketches for two high heels for the 'Space Shoe'. Although an extremely complicated design, the shoes sold out immediately. The sketches give a good impression of the spirit of the shoe.

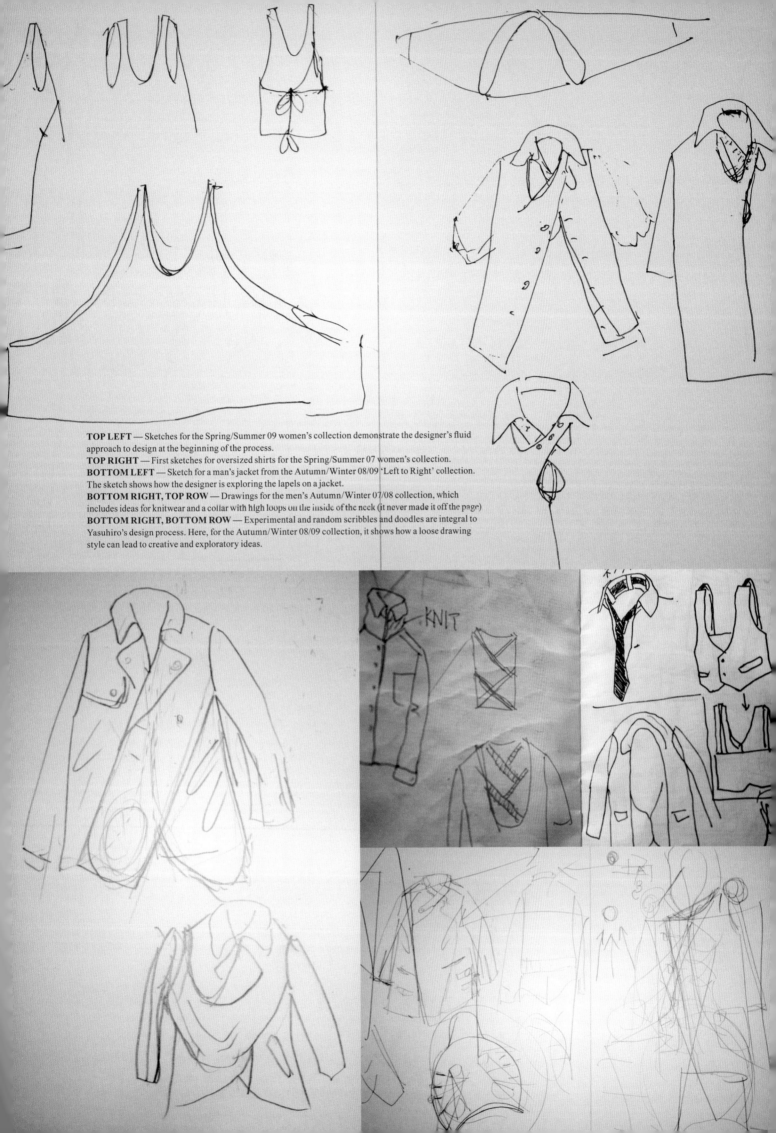

TOP LEFT — Sketches for the Spring/Summer 09 women's collection demonstrate the designer's fluid approach to design at the beginning of the process.

TOP RIGHT — First sketches for oversized shirts for the Spring/Summer 07 women's collection.

BOTTOM LEFT — Sketch for a man's jacket from the Autumn/Winter 08/09 'Left to Right' collection. The sketch shows how the designer is exploring the lapels on a jacket.

BOTTOM RIGHT, TOP ROW — Drawings for the men's Autumn/Winter 07/08 collection, which includes ideas for knitwear and a collar with high loops on the inside of the neck (it never made it off the page)

BOTTOM RIGHT, BOTTOM ROW — Experimental and random scribbles and doodles are integral to Yasuhiro's design process. Here, for the Autumn/Winter 08/09 collection, it shows how a loose drawing style can lead to creative and exploratory ideas.

Do you experience a 'eureka moment' when you know a design is working?

The moment usually comes at the late-night fittings when you see clothes coming together. Then I work on styling the show by taking images of our fittings and looking at the clothes and listening to the music I want to use for the show. You can't plan these 'eureka moments'. Themes can change at the last minute when the hair and make-up come together days before the show, but we sometimes move heaven and earth to make things work before the show.

How does your research and design work evolve from 2D to 3D?

It starts with the sketch; usually I am halfway around the world when I fax the sketches back to my team and they put the first prototypes in to work. These prototypes are made in substitute fabrics and that's when I see my ideas come to life. I also love to drape on the model – usually I have an idea in my head or something spontaneous comes up and I can see the cloth being draped on the body.

What are your sources of inspiration?

In the past, I've drawn themes from Procopius's Secret History – *the story of Empress Theodora – in which the feminine figure seduces her men. Much of my collection revolves around dressing this woman. However, I find that all the women I know, like Diane, my mother and even my little girl Lily are strong and inspiring. I design for them.*

How would you describe your design process?

I usually have a million ideas in my head; however, putting together a line requires a great degree of focus. I have a list of ideas and I jot down a lot of notes on my Blackberry about what I've seen travelling. I send those ideas to my design team and we meet to discuss how we should proceed with the season.

What is the best environment for you to work in?

It's weird, but I find working on a plane is the best place since I am by myself and there are not a million people around me and I cannot use my Blackberry.

Does your design process involve photography, drawing or reading?

NATHAN JENDEN

British Nathan Jenden studied at Central Saint Martins and then at the Royal College of Art. After **working for John Galliano, Kenzo and Daryl K, Jenden became creative director of Diane von Furstenberg in 2001. Following such exceptional experience in the industry, Jenden launched his own collection in 2006 to establish his personal design identity. He understands the need for wearable clothes but also possesses a creative edge that allows his designs to stand out.**

Do you have a team that is involved in the design process? If so, what do they do?

My team has to interpret my sketches with measurements and work closely with the sample makers and pattern makers to translate my concepts. It is very important to have a team who understand or 'get' you so they can make your vision happen. When I return to New York, I see these prototypes in fittings, and I further decide on the direction of the season.

Do you have sources of inspiration that you always revisit?

Although my influences range from 1950s couture to rave music, I always think about the structure for making tailored and beautiful clothes, and the attitude of the clothes on the body. Leaving aside all the styling, it is very important to create clothes that make a woman look desirable.

Is there a specific time of day when you are most creative?
I am a night owl, but aren't all creative types like that?

I constantly look to the past for inspiration from literature I've read or from some amazing historical figure. My Autumn/Winter 08/09 show was inspired by Tudor ladies of the court and by Henry VIII. This produced colours, such as gold and royal blue, and jewelled Venetian masks. For Spring/Summer 09, I was inspired by candles and the story of Alice in Wonderland, which led to clothes embellished with crazy origami and crystals.

Is there a routine to your design process?

I am usually exhausted by the end of each season, but after pulling off a show I head directly to Paris for Première Vision. I start off with the fabrics. I also have a sense of what the mood is. There could be a great movie I saw on a flight, or I could have seen a new exhibit in the city I'm in. A spark happens, and this leads to emails and phone calls to my design team in New York. A lot of research is done on mood and from looking at historical or contemporary images. A colour palette is compiled so we can start ordering fabrics and lab-dipping them in the colours of the season. We then make the samples of the clothes and that's where it all begins: the abstract ideas materialize into a formal plan for the season.

What materials are essential to your working methods?
I always need a thick pad of vellum paper and a Sharpie – you will always find them in my bags wherever I am travelling to and from.

Design sketches from Nathan Jenden's sketchbook show how the designer resolves ideas for a dress for his Autumn/Winter 08/09 collection. Quick sketches allow Jenden to experiment with design details and colour.

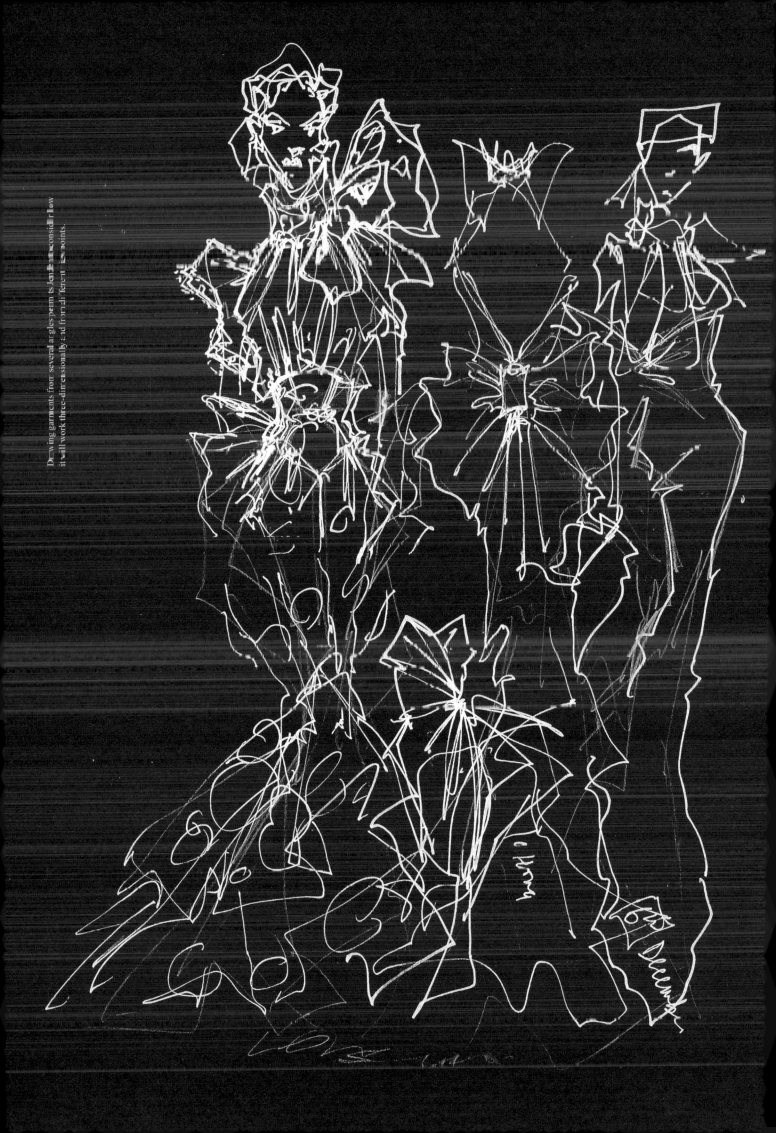

Drawing garments from several angles perm ts learning, consider low
it will work three-dimensionally and from different viewpoints.

Many design ideas generated through intensive sketching never make it past the page. These designs were all in development for Jenden's Autumn/Winter 08/09 collection, entitled 'The Secret History', but never made it into the show. The ideas are kept in a sketchbook and may be developed further in future seasons.

How important is research in your working process?

I am constantly looking at books, as my work is a lot about capturing volume in tailoring predominately inspired by ethnicity, so I am always surrounded by books.

How would you describe your design process?

I am a prolific sketcher; I work quite intensively and can sometimes do the main body of a collection over a short time. In a few days, I can do over a hundred drawings. Then I ponder over it and add or subtract.

What materials are essential to your working methods?

I use Moleskin books and normally an ink pen.

OSMAN YOUSEFZADA

Born in the UK to Afghani parents, Osman Yousefzada went into banking after graduating from Cambridge University in 1997. However, Yousefzada knew that his calling lay in fashion and decided to study fashion design at Central Saint Martins, graduating in 2003. Showing his collections at London Fashion Week, Yousefzada creates modern and glamorous clothes with an edge.

What is the most enjoyable part of designing for you?

I move on very quickly from one thing to another, as I have a short attention span and get bored quite easily. I hate overworking anything; some of the pieces that I look back at from past collections are those that are effortless. These are the ones that I still like, that are still strong for me. By the time a show comes, I have normally moved on to something else.

What fuels your design ideas?

There are always books on costume that I look at, and each time they inspire me differently.

Is there a routine to your design process?

It normally begins with sketching or draping my towel in the bathroom and looking at how it falls, and then working on the stand.

Is there a specific time of day when you are most creative?

Not really, it depends on how I feel generally.

Does your design process involve photography, drawing or reading?

In addition to sketching, a drape or fold could inspire me. I capture a lot of images on my iPhone camera as references. I am always looking for a mood.

What is the best environment for you to work in?

I work on trains, in hotel rooms, on my very messy small desk, at airports.

Do you experience a 'eureka moment' when you know a design is working?

This is normally at fitting, when you see the first toile work on the body; then you know you need more of this or less of that.

Do you have sources of inspiration that you always revisit?

Films are always key. Generally, I'm not limited to a set of things. Nature and colour are quite key to me.

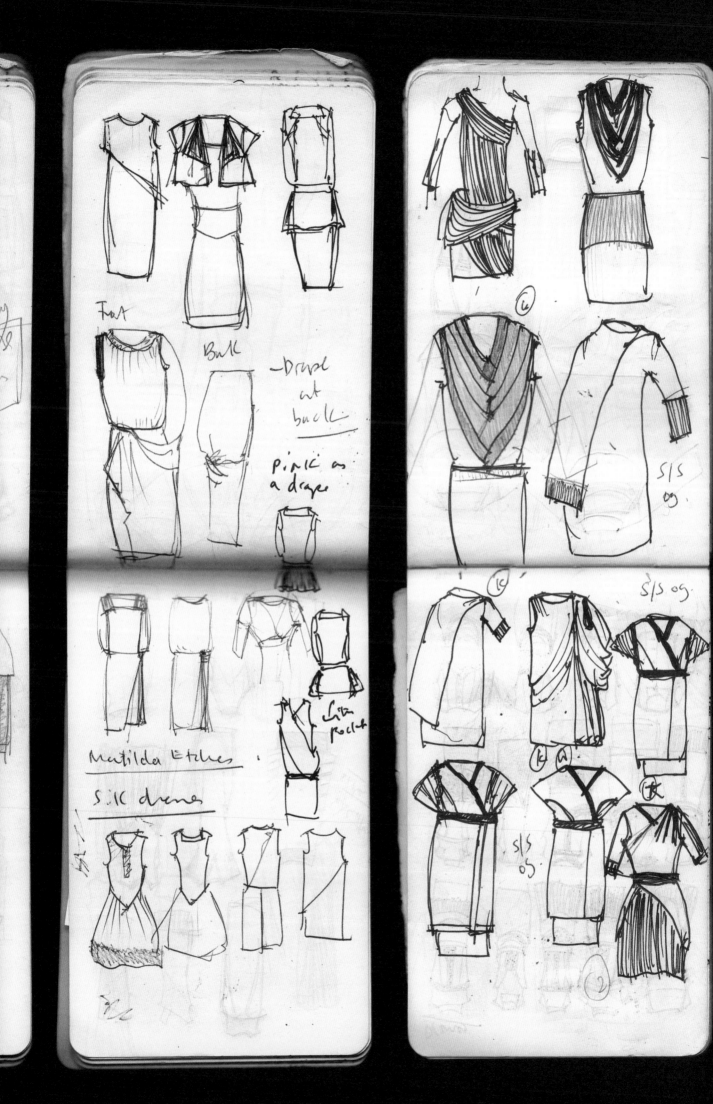

Fat

Back

—Drape
at
back

pink as
a drape

Matilda Etches

Silk dress

S/S
09.

S/S. 09.

S/S
09.

into
seam

PAGE 145 — Working drawings from Yousefzada's Autumn/Winter 08/09 sketchbook. The drawings show how the designer, in the early stages of the design process, explores different details and shapes for his collection entitled 'Celestial Migrants'.

Clear illustrations and a colour palette are created once the designs have been refined. These looks are from the 'Cosmic Mughal' collection for Autumn/Winter 09/10.

What materials are essential to your working methods?

I like to draw using a black fine-liner and white copier paper.

Do you experience a 'eureka moment' when you know a design is working?

Some designs come very easily and are the way you imagined them at every stage, while others can be hard work. Designs can change quite radically during the fittings, I think this is when you most often resolve the ones that aren't working, or realize that something is never going to work and needs to be binned.

What fuels your design ideas?

I always like there to be a bit of a story to each collection and I always have this idea of the muse, so I am always thinking about that.

How does your research and design work evolve from 2D to 3D?

Sometimes the inspiration is 3D if it comes from garments or objects, and so the design process can be 3D, for example, draping or a sewing technique. Other times, it's the pattern cutter who translates a drawing into a pattern.

Do you have sources of inspiration that you always revisit?

There are some photographers and artists whose work I come back to again and again. I particularly like photographers like Diane Arbus, August Sander, Weegee, Hans Eijkelboom; I often find inspiration in pictures, especially in this kind of documentary portraiture. I also find Cindy Sherman's work really inspiring; it's so much about creating characters through clothing, which is something I'm really interested in.

Is there a specific time of day when you are most creative?

I'm very much a morning person; I'm always at the studio by 8am at the latest. Apart from that, I like drawing at home on a Sunday while watching DVDs.

Born in Denmark, Peter Jensen trained in graphic design, embroidery and tailoring before studying fashion design at Central Saint Martins and graduating in 1999. He immediately launched a menswear line, the success of which saw Jensen create a womenswear line, and both are shown every season at London Fashion Week. His collections are eagerly anticipated each season as they signal future trends. With an individual and independent approach to fashion, Jensen fuses wit with desirable fashion.

PETER JENSEN

How important is research in your working process?

I think research is really important to the design process, but I can't really describe the process as it doesn't follow a set pattern. Sometimes I consciously do research, on a trip for instance or in the library; other times though I might see something inspiring on the TV or in the paper, or spot somebody in the street who is inspiring. It varies by collection as well. Sometimes I have a very specific idea about what the research process should be; for instance, for my A/W04/05 collection, I gathered together lots of my old garments and vintage pieces and invited friends to style and photograph outfits, and I used this as the research. Last season, we went on a trip to Greenland and we used the inspirations we found there to design the collection. Other collections can be inspired by lots of disparate things or a single image. I think it's quite difficult to design without any research, or without at least establishing some sort of boundary.

Is there a routine to your design process?

No, not really. Sometimes you know what kind of clothes you want to make and the process is about finding the research you need to help you make them. Other times, you don't know what you want to make at the beginning but just start researching something that interests you.

How would you describe your design process?

I guess there are lots of stages to the design. I tend to design garments individually rather than as whole outfits, so a lot of the look of the collection comes when it is put together for the show. I always have this idea of a muse that each collection is based on, sometimes she will be the starting point and sometimes she will come in later and tie it all together.

Do you have a team that is involved in the design process? If so, what do they do?

Yes, there is definitely a team. My partner, Gerard, is constantly involved in the design process: suggesting directions for the collection, selecting fabrics, the fittings and show production. Beth Fenton, the stylist I work with on the shows, is also very involved in developing the collection. This might mean bringing in found garments or images for reference, or sketching an interesting shoe she has just seen someone wearing on the street. She is also very important in putting together the show looks. I work with a textile designer on the prints as well, which is really important. There are lots of people involved really, everyone in the studio has some input, and even outside of that friends might suggest something or bring me garments or images that are inspirational.

What is the best environment for you to work in?

When I'm drawing I like to be alone, so maybe at home, but if I am dealing with fittings or selecting fabrics then I like to have other people around.

TOP — Design drawings by Peter Jensen show how the designer focuses on the shape of his garment. The three sketches show different variations on the same dress shape for his Spring/Summer 05 collection, entitled 'Tonya'.
BOTTOM — Fabric research for Jensen's Autumn/ Winter 09/10 'Jytte' collection. Fabric swatches are kept together to ensure the whole story works.

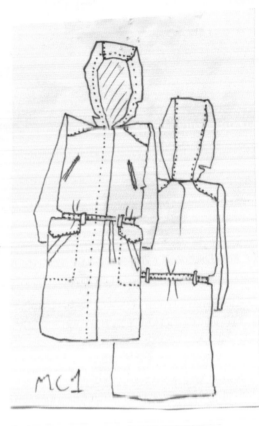

MC1

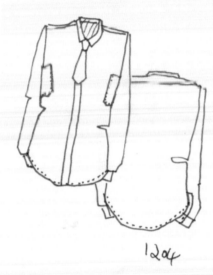

1204

Flat technical drawings, with front and back views, for the menswear Spring/Summer 08 'Mink' collection, showing how the garments are constructed.

441

8. CATO
9. VALENTIN
10. MEREL
11. ALEX
12. MARTHA

14. WILL
15. GIEDRE
16. LAURA
17. JILL
18. LYOKA

20. MELISSA
21. SARA
22. ANASTASIA
24. MYF

27. ALICE
28. MEREL
29. MARTHA
30. CATO

32. LAURA

Photographs of all the looks allow Jensen's team to create the running order for the Spring/Summer 09 show, 'Jodie', with clothes designed for the character Clarice Starling, played by Jodie Foster in *The Silence of the Lambs*. Photographs by Beth Fenton.

TOP LEFT — Flat design drawings for the Autumn/Winter 09/10 'Jytte' collection show what fabric will be used for the garment.
BOTTOM LEFT — Photographic research for the men's Spring/Summer 09 collection entitled 'Jodie', which included images of Adam Ant and historical tailoring.

TOP RIGHT — Drawings by Jensen for the Autumn/Winter 08/09 menswear collection entitled 'Keith'. The designer often depicts characters in his illustrations that define the mood of the collection.
BOTTOM RIGHT — Design drawings emphasize a detail on a skirt for Peter Jensen's 'Resort' Spring/Summer 10 collection.

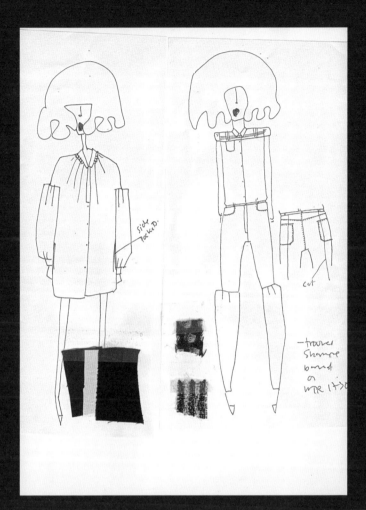

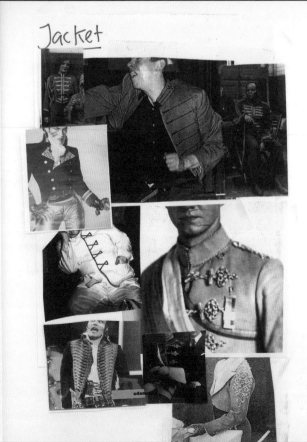

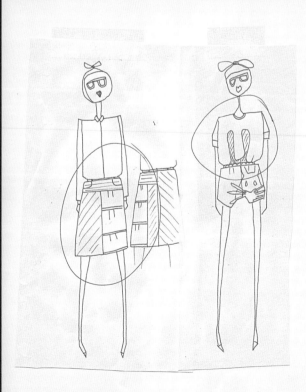

What is the most enjoyable part of designing for you?

The whole process is enjoyable. This helps, as when you spend all your time and love on something you have to be into it or else you're working for the wrong reasons.

How does your research and design work evolve from 2D to 3D?

I generally visualize designs in 3D and then work backwards. The rest of the team has to see 2D drawings until the first samples are made in the studio. We have a lot of visuals to work from, so it tends to be an enjoyable process.

What materials are essential to your working methods?

When we're designing, I'll always use black ink and have a small sketchbook on me all the time, but as ideas go you have to be able to deal with them how and any way they come to you. It's a myth that you can sit at a desk and it will happen. I can be having dinner and just have to stop and go and write something down. Or everything will come in one day. Final designs go on to loose sheets so they can be moved around and viewed as a group of designs, then ideas can be added or taken away. You develop a focus from being able to work anywhere.

What fuels your design ideas?

Films can be inspirational as can books, but you have to take them in your own direction.

Is there a specific time of day when you are most creative?

During the day we deal with sampling and new techniques for styles; then, in the evening, I'll get on with another level of what we have already achieved and try and push the process on, so it depends which part you see as more creative…the chicken or the egg.

Do you have a team that is involved in the design process? If so, what do they do?

We have a team that's involved in the research and construction of the sample collection. This is our design assistant and pattern-cutting team. We have a very good team and we all pull energy into the room – there's never room for the wrong type of attitude. They work on bringing to the table what's relevant for that season's theme, this is then dissected and we are left with the essence of what to go forward with.

Do you experience a 'eureka moment' when you know a design is working?

When we're having ideas, we generally know before going into too much depth whether they are good or not. You don't really discuss it, you just know if it's not turning you on; it's a pretty basic emotion.

Does your design process involve photography, drawing or reading?

Our design process starts with points of reference, ranging from fabrics, works of art, general objects, people or whatever we feel is relevant to the theme we are working towards. It can even be a statement from a friend that suddenly fits into the thought process in our minds. We have a large space for displaying inspiration, and make it new and fresh each season or for each project we are working on. Our studio is very busy always with several projects going on, as well as events and exhibitions that we are involved in.

PPQ

PPQ is a fashion label based in London. Founded in 1992 as a fashion, music and arts collective by Amy Molyneaux and Percy Parker, the PPQ clothing label was launched in 2000. PPQ offers 'luxe pop chic' and the collections are often inspired by music. In 2006 the design team opened their flagship store in London. The label is popular with musicians and bands as it offers young and wearable clothes that communicate the spirit of youth.

What is the best environment for you to work in?

We all work together in the studio every day, and this is usually our favourite place, but if I feel a wealth of ideas coming on I will retreat to my flat as I never know when the doorbell is going to ring and everyone will pile in.

How would you describe your design process?

Our design process has always been attached to our lifestyle. We work all the time on our designs, it's not like a job where we get up and go to work. We live in the PPQ environment we have created. On a normal day, we work all day on PPQ and then more than likely have an event or night to go to…then do it all again the next day.

How important is research in your working process?

Research can be in the form of mood boards, nights out or a trip away somewhere. It's a complete creative process where nothing is left out of the equation. Then, when we're ready, we will be very specific about our print direction and colours, and this is how the collection is born.

Do you have sources of inspiration that you always revisit?

Percy and I inspire each other. We constantly talk about new ways and new things. Sometimes it's fraught, other times it's hilarious. We revisit moments in time when we had an experience that could be what we're looking for now, for example, an event we had or a place we visited that we can look at again to see why it was something we were into.

A design drawing for a multicoloured 'Paloma' long dress for the Autumn/Winter 09/10 collection. The drawing illustrates the spirit of the collection, while the fabric swatches show how the patchwork pattern will be constructed on the dress. A side and back view of the outfit communicates the long silhouette of the garment.

All over
Patchwork
design.

A design drawing for the 'Ypris' all-in-one red jumpsuit for PPQ's Autumn/Winter 09/10 collection. A fabric swatch is attached to the drawing, which also illustrates details for the accompanying accessory.

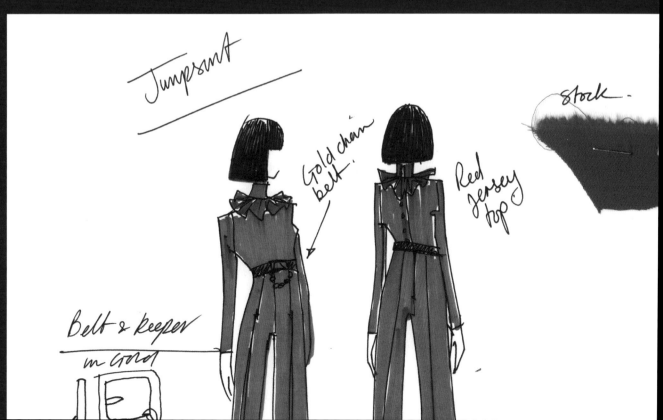

Jumpsuit

Gold chain
belt.

Stock.

Red
Jersey
top

Belt & keeper
in Gold

British-born Richard Nicoll was raised in Australia before going to study in London. He graduated from Central Saint Martins in 2002. After working with Marc Jacobs at Louis Vuitton, Nicoll launched his own collection in 2005 and since has presented his collections at London Fashion Week. Nicoll has been lauded by the fashion press for his individual approach to modern clothes and his unique, creative and fresh vision.

RICHARD NICOLL

What is the best environment for you to work in?

I like to work on planes where there are no distractions; they are always the place where I lay down the skeleton ideas for the collection.

Does your design process involve photography, drawing or reading?

My design process involves all of the above plus a lot of talking and trying out ideas through collage and then through making toiles. The designs continue to evolve throughout the course of the collection, I never draw something and that is it. There has to be a continual process of trial and error to achieve the best result.

How does your research and design work evolve from 2D to 3D?

Almost immediately after doing my initial sketches, I start to produce the basic silhouette shapes. For me, the sooner I start in 3D, the better the finished design, otherwise it remains theoretical.

How important is research in your working process?

Research is very important – it defines and reflects the themes of the collection – and could be an image or even just a conversation or analysis of themes.

Is there a routine to your design process?

Yes. Once the research is done, I think of a way to structure the outfits into a running order from look 1 to 31, or however many outfits I am doing. I don't like to make pieces randomly that don't fit into a specific look as I worry about wasting money and time...each piece has to play an important role in the jigsaw. Once I have done this, I start to make toiles and photograph the first fitting, which I then print out and draw and colour over the top of. This process continues as the collection evolves until we photograph final looks for the show with finished pieces on the fit model. We are then ready for the models to try on their looks the night before the show.

What materials are essential to your working methods?

Just a ream of A4 paper, a tracing pad, a set of Uni Pin fine-liner pens in black and a template of naked girls that I use from a Jock Sturges book.

How would you describe your design process?

The process for me is quite structured: I choose a mood or feeling to base the collection on, then find visual and audio references that reflect the mood or feeling, then start sketching, make basic shapes and finally refine the idea through the course of the fittings and fabrication.

Do you experience a 'eureka moment' when you know a design is working?

When I design the running order and it makes sense as a story on paper from look 1 to 31 without any randomness, that is when I feel excited and ready to start the toiles.

Is there a specific time of day when you are most creative?

I'm freshest first thing in the morning, at around 7am, when I can work alone in the studio before staff, phone calls and emails appear.

What fuels your design ideas?

I buy a lot of photography books for reference, but the inspiration can come from anywhere: a mood, a feeling, a smell, an atmosphere, a person on the street, a conversation, a piece of art, a philosophy. Mostly, image research is there to communicate the idea to the rest of the team.

Do you have a team that is involved in the design process? If so, what do they do?

My friends Meera Sleight and Anthony Campbell act as consultants. I talk with them about ideas and they help me with research if I have a lot on. Equally, my assistant Ben Mazey and pattern cutters help me with decision-making during fittings. My stylist Jacob K and casting director Russell Marsh help me with the look of the girls. I love having many people involved.

What is the most enjoyable part of designing for you?

The best parts are the drawing phase, the final making of the toiles and the realization stage, when things start to look believable. The process in-between is the most punishing because that is the phase that I am least involved in – when I'm waiting for pattern cutters and machinists to produce first toiles, etc.

Do you have sources of inspiration that you always revisit?

I have an ideal that I always revisit, which is one of celebrating the idiosyncratic and the individual. I like a mix of ideas; I guess I always make a collection that is a 'collage' of different and opposing themes.

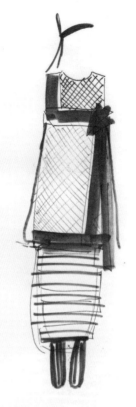

Development sketches by Nicoll for his Autumn/Winter 08/09 collection. The apparently simple line drawings, in black and white, give a clear indication of the design of the garments. A thicker pen stroke is used to emphasize key details on the garments.

Sequin trimmed bodice

Polka Print?

Some sequins

Drawing with design notes for a freelance project by Nicoll. The illustration uses photographic image to give an energetic mood and atmosphere to the garment.

embroidered
Slogan
port Shirt

Patchwork
poplin
Dress
w
Metal
embroidery

Raffia &
Ribbon
embellished
embroidered
Slogan
bodice

Raffia
& Ribbon
Underskirt
on dress.

Raffia
Ribbon S

⑤ ⑥ ⑨ ⑩

Is there a routine to your design process?
Well, it always starts with research, then design, then development into 3D, but we wouldn't say that there is a path or a method. Of course, we have to work in a certain way, as we can't go backwards, but we tend to be very relaxed about the process and like to give ourselves not too many time limitations at any given stage of the process, hence making it as organic as possible.

What fuels your design ideas?
As mentioned, anything can fuel our process, it really depends on what we are feeling is relevant to today, and what feels right. That said, we are creating a brand and an image, so we are creating a vision that hopefully people want to be part of. For us, the Teddy boy and rockabilly movements are extremely interesting, as we love the way the tailoring has such an important and almost aggressive subcontext, so this is something we always go back to, which also gives us a continuous aesthetic to work on and develop.

What is the most enjoyable part of designing for you?
We love researching and getting deep into topics. It really opens our eyes on how we can go about things, not only designing clothes, but fabrics, textures and above all creating an interesting atmosphere.

What materials are essential to your working methods?
Just a black pen and white paper – anything more and the design process becomes something uptight and unnecessary.

What are your sources of inspiration?
Everything and anything can inspire us. It can be something as small as a trim found at a vintage fair or as grand as an important painting or film. The best way to find it is not to look for it.

How important is research in your working process?
We feel research is paramount when designing a collection and we put a great amount of energy into it. For us, it's the most exciting part of the design process – nothing's set in stone and any direction is possible.

Is there a specific time of day when you are most creative?
Yes, at night. It brings us certain calmness.

Of Anglo-Indian descent, Fiona Sinha was born in Aberdeen and raised in Newcastle. Aleksandar Stanic was born in Croatia and moved to Hamburg,

SINHA—STANIC

Germany, in 1990. Together they form Sinha—Stanic, a fashion label based in London. In 1998, both designers moved to London to begin courses at Central Saint Martins. Sinha studied a BA in Womenswear Fashion Design, while Stanic studied a BA in Fashion Design and Print. Graduating in 2002, they launched their first collection in 2004 and entered the Fashion Fringe competition. As one of four finalists, Sinha—Stanic debuted their collection at London Fashion Week. After the show, they signed with Aeffe, the Italian luxury-goods company. Their first independent show took place at London Fashion Week in February 2005.

Does your design process involve photography, drawing or reading?
Yes, our process involves all these things. Some collections are heavily influenced by photography, while others may draw influence from films or even a single painting.

How would you describe your design process?
Organic and continuous.

What is the best environment for you to work in?
Usually it is at home on the weekends. The studio can get very hectic, with the phones ringing all day, and you tend to work on everything else except what matters.

How does your research and design work evolve from 2D to 3D?
It depends, we tend to spend a long time researching and changing our ideas about what we are doing. We don't like to turn things into 3D until we know we are happy with our concept. When we finally start turning our research and designs into actual pieces, the concept may change, and that's OK, but the initial idea has to be right for us to commit to turn something into 3D.

Do you experience a 'eureka moment' when you know a design is working?
There is certainly an exciting moment when we realize that a piece has worked out the way we hoped, or even better, and everyone that has worked on it has a certain satisfaction about them. It is definitely a very happy but sadly short-lived moment!

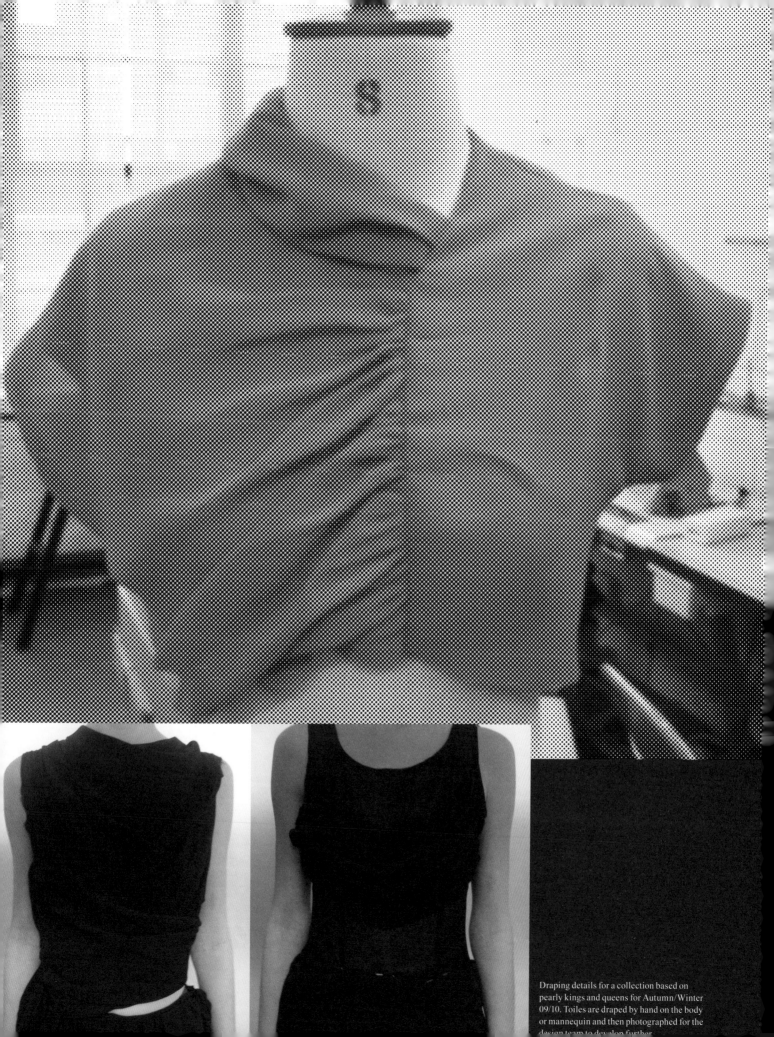

Draping details for a collection based on
pearly kings and queens for Autumn/Winter
09/10. Toiles are draped by hand on the body
or mannequin and then photographed for the
design team to develop further.

TOP LEFT — First toiles for a stripy tone-on-tone knitted dress for the Autumn/Winter 08/09 collection.
TOP MIDDLE & RIGHT — The first toiles for a stripy black and cream knitted cardigan for the Autumn/Winter 08/09 collection, based on the American TV series *Freaks & Geeks*.

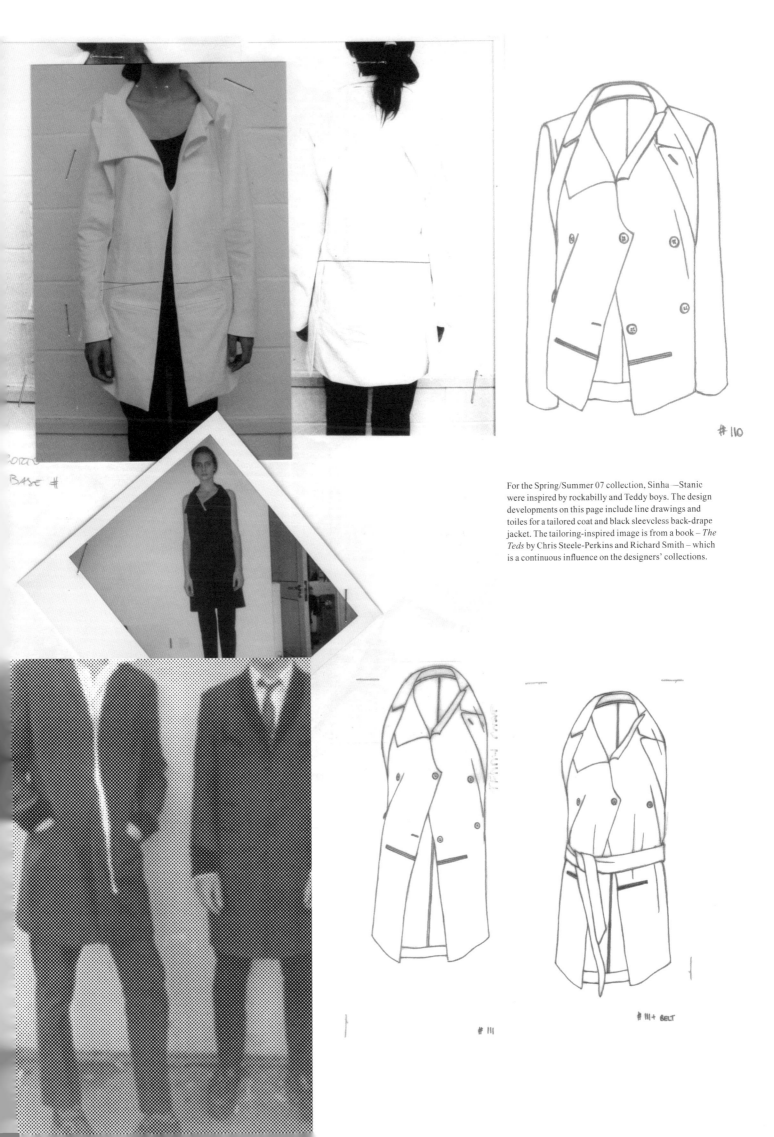

110

For the Spring/Summer 07 collection, Sinha —Stanic were inspired by rockabilly and Teddy boys. The design developments on this page include line drawings and toiles for a tailored coat and black sleevcless back-drape jacket. The tailoring-inspired image is from a book – *The Teds* by Chris Steele-Perkins and Richard Smith – which is a continuous influence on the designers' collections.

111

111 + BELT

Is there a specific time of day when you are most creative?

In the afternoon and evening. I also work through a lot in my sleep and often wake up because I need to write something down or make a quick sketch.

What is the most enjoyable part of designing for you?

I enjoy each part of the process a lot; it is a real pleasure to dive into and drive a project forward. I set aside about half the time to research it. I spend a lot of time gathering information as I have to collect enough to react to it, and then the design process goes very quickly. When the research comes together, I design the collection on paper in a few days, but the design process does not stop on paper for me. When we start making things up I enjoy having the freedom to still react to things that come up, so I guess the design process is not finished until the garment has been completed.

Norwegian Siv Støldal is a menswear designer who graduated from Central Saint Martins in 1999. Støldal has shown her collections in London and Paris and has collaborated with Fred Perry and Topman. In 2006, the British Fashion Council nominated Støldal as Menswear Designer of the Year. Her idiosyncratic approach to design incorporates unusual research techniques and displays, and her clothes often tell the story of their evolution. Støldal has developed a reputation for creating carefully thought-out pieces that while appealing to the wearer in their casualness also offer a narrative that enhances their desirability.

SIV STØLDAL

What materials are essential to your working methods?

I work on regular white A4 copy paper, and I need a 0.1 and a 0.5 black Pilot pen, Tippex, a pencil and a white rubber. Other than that, I need my photographs printed out and access to a copy machine.

What are your sources of inspiration?

My inspiration is always first-hand information that I collect myself by interviewing, photographing and writing. I very rarely use books or films in my research, but something I see on TV or an article or a photograph in the newspaper can pop up perhaps. It is always funny to see where this information takes you; when you have set your mind on a certain theme, you discover things in conversations, when reading the paper or watching TV that you would have been blind to before. In the 'Three Wardrobes' project, I interviewed a group of Norwegian men who say they are not interested in their clothing. I photographed every garment they own and collected stories and facts about each piece. What came out were the very personal attachment stories that they in fact have with their clothes, and each man's personal clothing passion manifests itself. This way, I have discovered the very beautiful conceptual thoughts that we can have about clothing, and I feel very honoured the men shared them with me.

What is the best environment for you to work in?

Is there a routine to your design process?

Yes, I guess I have found a path. Through experience, I know the journey from research to collection well and have a good idea where I am in the process at a given time. Saying that, I like challenging myself within the process by doing things differently. Creative blocks happen, which of course are hard, but I know these moments of hitting a wall are necessary to work through the layers and to get deeper into the material in the research.

I always thought I needed to be in the studio and also quite alone with loud music. But lately I have also spent time in my local library in Norway. Lots of old ladies work there and they have made this little, very granny-like, area in the back, with a 1950s sofa and mismatched chairs and a table, really cute embroidered pillows and random flea-market lamps. It is very 'granny', and I really like to work there. It is mostly quiet, but once in a while these funny ladies come by and comment on what I design.

Do you experience a 'eureka moment' when you know a design is working?

Sure. Things that are exciting and surprise me in the research are always the best, and I always pick up on one of the really exciting aspects to work with first. Then, later in the process, I know I have something when what is on the paper or on the garment in front of me is something I have never seen before. I believe it is a designer's job and pleasure to make garments that are new to the world and when this happens their appearance surprises the viewer; they are always a bit stupid and make me laugh. Then I know there is something that I like.

How does your research and design work evolve from 2D to 3D?

For me, the whole process is always 3D, I never see it as 2D. I have a strong background as a tailor and have a lot of knowledge about making and patterns. So I guess I am always thinking about ideas in a very solution-oriented way, and since the process both starts with research on clothing and finishes with actual clothing, the research and work process can sometimes feel abstract but never 2D to me.

How would you describe your design process?

The design process starts when I have collected enough research for me to consider it: I categorize, dissect, mix things up and comment on the process through the clothes, sunglasses, shoes. I design.

For the 'Three Wardrobes' project for Autumn/Winter 09/10, Siv Støldal interviewed a pensioner who owned 16 trench coats. The coats all had variations of the same 'trench' details and colours, but none were identical. This led to the idea of making 'two coats in one', where each side represents two different coats.

Knit samples are used to inform shapes for clothes. Garments found in Støldal's grandparents' summerhouse in Hardanger, Norway, inspired these jumpers from her Central Saint Martins MA Menswear graduate collection in 1999.

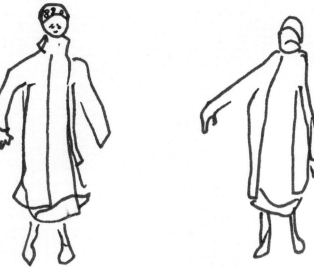

For Støldal's 'Scarecrow' Autumn/Winter 01/02 collection, the
designer researched the idea of unconscious dressing, asking people
from seven houses on her home island of Tyssøy to make a scarecrow.
Støldal documented the work, which informed her collection.

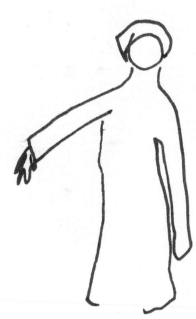

For the 'Trace' Autumn/Winter 03/04 collection, Støldal photographed inhabitants of the island of Tyssøy in
Norway, documenting their idea of the term 'Sunday best'. She transferred each of the pictures on to cloth, and
then made small sculptures of each inhabitant, which became her starting point for designing garments.

Studies for knitwear for Støldal's first collection called 'Bob James', for Spring/Summer 01. The starting point was four jumpers the designer wore as a child.

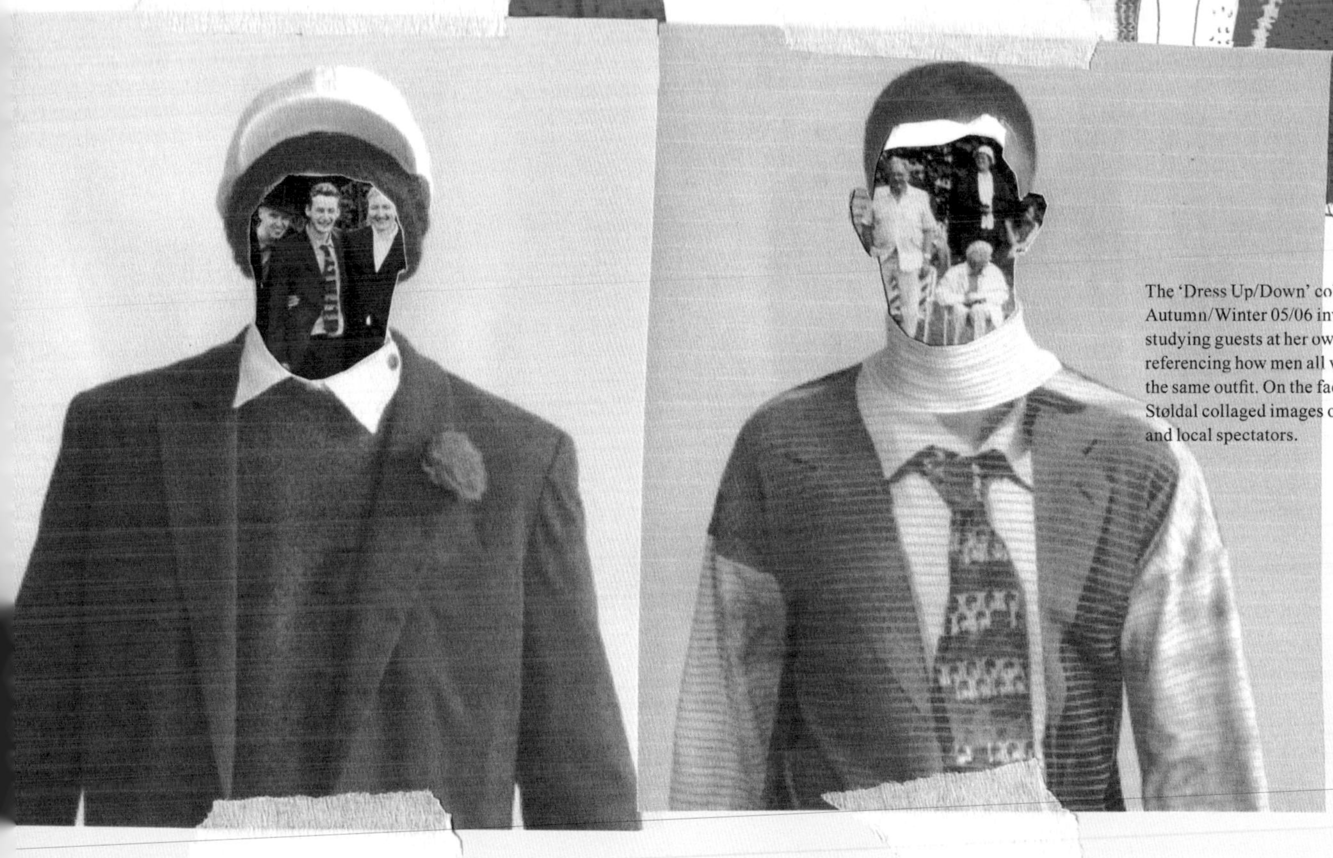

The 'Dress Up/Down' collection for Autumn/Winter 05/06 involved the designer studying guests at her own wedding and referencing how men all wear variations of the same outfit. On the faces of the models, Støldal collaged images of wedding guests and local spectators.

double
pashmina

A sketchbook page from Støldal's MA Menswear collection in 1999.
'I used to sketch a lot on the bus and on the tube in those days and this
page is a mix of all this,' explains the designer.

Does your design process involve photography, drawing or reading?

It involves a lot of drawing and painting. This is the part that takes the longest time and involves huge concentration and attention to detail. It's the part that whatever happens we always do ourselves, and is best done when it's just Toshio and me working alone in the studio. We also take pictures, often of things we find that we know we might draw later or use somehow. We also use, of course, all the pictures of Candy our dog as she often features in our prints, sometimes in a big way and sometimes as a tiny detail like a hard-to-find miniature. I am a little embarrassed to say we do have a very large gallery of photographs of Candy.

How does your research and design work evolve from 2D to 3D?

As soon as the fabrics arrive. We have patterns and shapes literally waiting on the table, and from then on the storm begins and it's chaos and late nights until we finish!

Do you have sources of inspiration that you always revisit?

There are particular books that we often revisit, botanical drawings especially. And, perhaps a visit to The Wallace Collection, in particular to see the tiny miniature watercolours on ivory. To be honest though, each season we always have a lot of new references and inspiration as we have been collecting all the books, images, photographs and objects that we plan to use.

Is there a specific time of day when you are most creative?

Not really, although often we work in the evening or over the weekend as there are less emails arriving to distract us.

What is the most enjoyable part of designing for you?

There is not really a part of the design process that we don't like. There are difficult parts when we struggle to find what we want to do and to feel like we have got to a point where we are happy, but this is all part of designing something. The most enjoyable part is laying out all the drawings and feeling like you have found the perfect design. The other really exciting days are receiving the fabrics from our printer; this is so exciting and we all just stand around trying them on and talking about them.

How would you describe your design process?

We begin by finding the theme or the objects that we will work with to create the collection. From there, we start the drawings and paintings, the lengthiest part of the process. We then put the drawings together into prints or scarves, again, this is quite a painstaking process involving lots of changes and rethinks. Then we send all the designs off to print and sit here in anticipation of the result. After some proofs and technical changes, we receive the final fabrics. By this point, we are clear about exactly what these will become and it's a matter of working very hard and very quickly to bring the collection together.

Do you experience a 'eureka moment' when you know a design is working?

Yes, there is definitely a moment when you know something's working, and from that moment you also know the exact next thing you want to work on.

Swash is a fashion-design partnership based in London. Sarah Swash and Toshio Yamanaka both studied fashion design at Central Saint Martins before forming the label. Initially selling their designs in Japan, they went

SWASH

on to win acclaim in Europe after taking three prizes, including the Grand Prix, at the nineteenth Festival International des Arts de la Mode at Hyères in 2004. Swash's clothes rely on the idea of collaboration between the designers, and their design style often explores how shape, print and multifunctional uses can be employed.

How important is research in your working process?

It plays a big part, especially in the drawings and the fact that each print we make has quite a distinctive theme. Our design process begins when we contemplate what to do and where to start. This is always supposed to be relatively brief but always takes far longer than we planned. It basically means gathering together things that we like, books mainly. We spend ages wandering around bookshops and quite often antique and junk shops, where we might find a drawing or an old book that takes us in a new direction. Once we have that, it's easier to move and research one or two particular subjects in more depth.

Is there a routine to your design process?

Yes: research, gather, draw, paint, scan, design, pattern cut and then wait for the fabrics.

What fuels your design ideas?

Everything really, as it's so much about gathering all the small things together that we will use to create the look and direction of the collection. We might take ideas about colour from books or a film or a photograph we have taken some time before, and we might use these same or completely different books or objects for the drawings. Gathering these resources is one of the most enjoyable parts of being a designer as it's about discovering things, gathering objects and ideas, and is an incredible excuse just to look at, read about and discover things that excite us creatively.

What materials are essential to your working methods?

A Pilot G-Tec-C4 pen, that's the only one Toshio will draw with. Also, Winsor & Newton watercolour paints and a particular weight of Daler Rowney paper.

Paper pattern pieces show all the components that will be translated into
fabric for a 'Whippet coat' for Swash's Spring/Summer 10 collection.

Simple strokes of watercolour provide the colour reference for Swash's Spring/Summer 09 collection.

OPPOSITE — Drawing is an essential part of Swash's design process as it informs the print design on garments. 'The drawings and paintings are done at our studio or at home,' explain the designers. 'The most important things to get these done are peace, quiet and vitally a deadline, as otherwise we could spend forever on them.' Drawings by Toshio Yamanaka for Swash's Spring/Summer 09 collection.

What materials are essential to your working methods?

My sketchbook, the so-called book of truth, is always at my side, as it not only gathers my sketches and thoughts but it is also my external drawer for collecting pictures, pieces of fabric and other items.

How would you describe your design process?

My design process starts with filtering my day-to-day reality: my walks through the city, my conversations, images, a representation of a feeling, an important shape or object or sometimes just a colour. These stills I capture in a drawing or in my head. I start collecting images from magazines, adding colours and putting this loose collection into shape in one of my books or on a mood board. My collections are a constant flow, coming from the same source. They are a work in progress and could be seen as a whole entity.

How important is research in your working process?

Research takes up a big part of my day-to-day living because it happens constantly, most of the time without me knowing. I want my collections to be personal, therefore I do not separate my personal life and my work. I live like a silent observer and absorb like a sponge.

Do you have sources of inspiration that you always revisit?

I have certain people in my close entourage, my muses, who inspire me. Observing them, just being with them, makes me want to make clothes for them to wear. Others, I meet out of the blue – crazy geniuses, sparkling minds, just random characters. When it comes to objects or styles, I think I will always love the simple and used.

What is the best environment for you to work in?

I can work and sleep anywhere, but I feel most comfortable when I am alone somewhere in my many retreats. I love to work in Spain, or Ibiza where I grew up.

TILLMANN LAUTERBACH

German-born Tillmann Lauterbach was raised in Ibiza. In 2000, after working for Deutsche Bank for two years, he realized that his interest lay in fashion. He studied at ESMOD in Paris and graduated in 2003 with a Diploma in Fashion Design and Pattern Cutting. He worked for Plein Sud in Paris before launching his own label in 2005. Lauterbach's design philosophy is to create collections that are understated and made of the finest fabrics.

What is the most enjoyable part of designing for you?

Every part of the process is enjoyable, every part is different and every part can turn out to be a real hassle, depending on my state of mind. An artist has the luxury to wait the time it takes until an idea is ripe, but a fashion designer has to force the process in order to meet his deadline. We are craftsmen, just one of many wheels in a machine, therefore we can't allow ourselves the luxury of time or pace as we know our delay will slow down everyone involved in the process, resulting in an unfinished collection, aka a disaster.

Is there a specific time of day when you are most creative?

My actual designing, bringing the ideas to paper happens mostly at night, as it is the only moment of the day when the phone is quiet and I am all by myself in the studio.

Do you have a team that is involved in the design process? If so, what do they do?

I design 100% of the collections and accessories myself, but I send out my personal assistant for specific research. My close circle of friends, my emotional family, also provides me with catalogues from exhibitions. Every collection happens in a different way, with different people involved.

Do you experience a 'eureka moment' when you know a design is working?

There are many states in the process that are very satisfying. There are moments of solitude when the jigsaw falls into place, when the idea of what the collection is all about becomes reality. There are moments of surprise and amazement when the first piece is made with definite fabric and trimmings. And, there is the moment of exhaustion and magic when the show is over and I look into all the faces that made it happen, all these people who actually make 'me', and whose love and devotion makes that ship called 'collection' sail.

Tillmann Lauterbach uses abstract references to inspire his collections. Colour,
light and texture can inform the designs of his garments. Photographs and
illustrations by Tillmann Lauterbach inspired the Spring/Summer 08 collection.

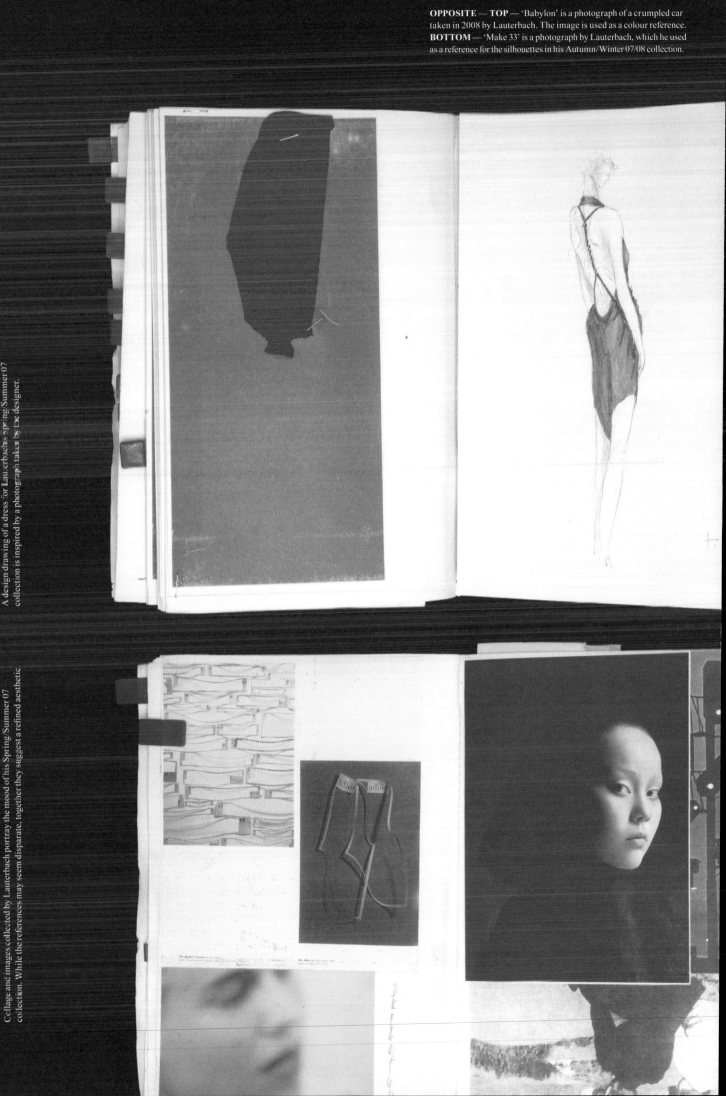

A design drawing of a dress for Lauterbach's Spring/Summer 07 collection is inspired by a photograph taken by the designer.

Collage and images collected by Lauterbach portray the mood of his Spring/Summer 07 collection. While the references may seem disparate, together they suggest a refined aesthetic

Does your design process involve photography, drawing or reading?
Yes, more drawing and reading.

What is the best environment for you to work in?
On a plane or trapped in a hotel room with no interruptions.

How important is research in your working process?
Research comes from everything and anything: news, books, film, travel. It's a strong reaction to what is going on in the world and an optimistic look towards the future.

Is there a routine to your design process?
No, it always changes. It has to.

TIM HAMILTON

Designer Tim Hamilton was born in Iowa to a Lebanese mother and an Anglo-American father. He founded his label in 2007 and his design studio is based in New York, from where he sells to stores throughout the USA, Europe and Asia. He has been nominated three times (2007, 2008 and 2009) for the Council of Fashion Designers of America's Swarovski Award for Menswear. Recognizing a gap in the men's market for luxury sportswear, Hamilton is a key figure in New York's new wave of menswear designers.

What fuels your design ideas?
They come from everywhere: books, newspaper clippings, an image from a film, a person. Anything can inspire or trigger the concept.

How would you describe your design process?
It's fast-paced with lots of thought. It's a challenge to make things modern, and I am always trying to simplify things. The formula is: concept in head, fabric, sketch, proto, fit, show.

What materials are essential to your working methods?
Dry paper and felt-tip markers. The pens I like are Micron 05 for inking all of the sketches and flats.

Do you experience a 'eureka moment' when you know a design is working?
At times, but how you envision it on paper doesn't always translate on to a garment.

Do you have sources of inspiration that you always revisit?
Fabric. Newness is fabric.

Is there a specific time of day when you are most creative?
When I can't sleep.

PAGE 181 — TOP — Abstract references for colour and mood are collated from tear sheets for Hamilton's Spring/Summer 10 collection.
BOTTOM — Space is a key reference for the Spring/Summer 10 collection and inspirational imagery is mounted to concept boards to inspire the design team.

TOP — 'Flats' or flat line drawings of the Spring/Summer 10 collection are displayed on Tim Hamilton's studio wall allowing a quick reference guide.
BOTTOM — A white shirt toile is fitted on a mannequin.

What fuels your design ideas?

If I am not creating I am unhappy. That's fuel enough for me.

How important is research in your working process?

Research is crucial and happens at every level research into fabric, manufacturers and techniques is just as important as design research.

Do you have sources of inspiration that you always revisit?

We all constantly revisit the same things in our lives. Design is no different. You mine your inspiration, look at it from different viewpoints, try to deconstruct it, but essentially you are still dealing with the same thing. After a while, unless you are exceptional, you start to repeat yourself. Then, it is time to move on!

London-based menswear designer Tim Soar has a diverse background in music, graphics and Interiors. In 2005, Soar launched his fashion label, which is defined by a minimalist and avant-garde approach. Soar's first collection was bought by London's B-Store and the second collection by Liberty. Considered as seriously modern menswear, Soar's clothes are well fitting and beautifully constructed. With tailoring at the forefront of his ideas, Soar also adds an experimental element to his designs.

TIM SOAR

Do you experience a 'eureka moment' when you know a design is working?

Fashion is certainly a more complex process than most other design disciplines – that is definitely the case as a small independent designer. The finished garment is THE product. So you might have a great 'eureka moment', send everything off to the factory and then it comes back looking like a sack of shit. I am sure every designer has horror stories like this. Therefore, the only time a design really works is when all the disparate elements come together in one garment or look.

What are your sources of inspiration?

This is going to sound a little cheesy, but because I am fairly old and have been involved in many different aspects of design and music over the years, I have built a large repository of stuff. This is particularly true of fashion. I have loved, bought and worn interesting clothes for well over thirty years. The memories of all these different things act as my main design repository. Youth has energy, age has experience; you work with what you have.

Do you have a team that is involved in the design process? If so, what do they do?

Yes, indeed. I think it is really important to include the team in the process. I work with a small team of interns each season. Some have great ideas, some are not so strong, but I give time to each one. If they are prepared to work long and hard for nothing, then I am most certainly going to let them put their ideas on the table. It might be as simple as a team vote on a feature or garment or they might come to me with a specific idea. The reason for this is not just altruistic. Fashion design at any level past the small artisan designer is a collaborative process. If you can't get past your own ego, you are never going to be able to grow your label. Most importantly, I work very closely with my stylist Jodie Barnes. I always listen to what he has to say. Jodie's input is there from the beginning of the collection. One of the key pieces of advice I would give to any new designer is get a good stylist. I am lucky, Jodie is one of the best.

What materials are essential to your working methods?

A computer, an Internet connection and 'CmdShft3'. To clarify, much of my research comes from the Internet, particularly eBay. It is a godsend. It is like the largest clothing museum in the world.

My research happens in two ways. Firstly, I have a very large collection of old garments from all periods. I look at these for mood inspiration as much as anything else. Once that mood is established, I will then look for photographic references. Secondly, at the beginning of the season I make a lot of small toiles, looking at different construction and technical details. I then combine these two things in Photoshop 'sketches' or Illustrator drawings.

What is the best environment for you to work in?

A messy little nook, but as I have said I think it is good to shake things up a bit, so it feels like it is due the chop. Sorry nook.

Does your design process involve photography, drawing or reading?

Is there a specific time of day when you are most creative?

It can be any time.

How does your research and design work evolve from 2D to 3D?

I try to work in 3D as soon as possible. Good menswear, for me, is about a combination of fit, fabric, design idea and detailing. So, the sooner you start working in 3D, the sooner you know whether the design idea is going to work with all the other elements.

How would you describe your design process?

My design process is about looking at moods, techniques and volumes. I hate to use the word 'organic' but the process is, for want of a better word, organic. My collections evolve over the whole design and sampling period, and it is often not until the last minute that I can stand back and see all the themes and influences.

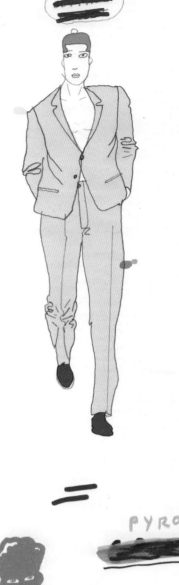

'Illustrator Paul Davis has been a good friend for many years. I have always admired his ability to distil down the essence of the human condition into seemingly simple images. I asked Paul to do some drawings of my Spring/Summer 09 collection as I wanted something a bit different from the usual photographs,' explains Tim Soar. SOAR/Davis illustrations.

In parallel with
the technical toiles,
Soar experiments
by making collages
in Photoshop.
'These collages
are not intended to
be direct images of
possible garments,
rather they are used
to get an idea of
overall mood.'
Shown here is a
jacket idea for the
Spring/Summer
10 collection.

TOP — Collar experimentation for Spring/Summer 10. Soar was inspired by paper folding and origami and wanted to explore an angular folded feel for many of the pieces

BOTTOM — Shirt front and back experimentation for the Spring/Summer 10 collection. 'I do not really start with strong narrative themes at the beginning of a collection,' explains Soar. 'I have general moods and silhouettes in mind, and there will be ideas from previous seasons that I want to explore further. Very early on I will do quick technical toiles to play with ideas.'

What fuels your design ideas?
I studied at a school in Graz, Austria, and it was an arty town with more art house cinemas than in London. This was in the late 1970s and 1980s, and I was a curious youth and watched everything there was. I think these influences stayed in my memory and I continue to use them as a source of inspiration.

Do you have sources of inspiration that you always revisit?
The human body. You dress eventually to be naked, so you want to look sexy and beautiful and to express yourself. I like looking at portraits by painters such as Gainsborough, to look at the subjects in the portraits and how the clothes communicate with the observer.

Do you have a team that is involved in the design process? If so, what do they do?
Of course I have a team that I work with and they help to fulfil my ideas. I work a lot with young people and I encourage them to be free and to think organically.

VIVIENNE WESTWOOD

Iconic British designer Vivienne Westwood has influenced the global fashion industry with her challenging and progressive approach to fashion design. Infamous for inventing punk through her partnership with Malcolm McLaren, Westwood has always pushed and questioned what is tasteful and appropriate in contemporary dress. Her husband, Andreas Kronthaler, is now creative director of the fashion brand. Vivienne Westwood's approach to design remains avant-garde, provocative and brave.

How does your research and design work evolve from 2D to 3D?
I'm completely 3D. My first attempt is 3D as I drape immediately on the mannequin. For me, 2D doesn't give a sense of the item as it appears on the body, whereas in 3D the piece is present in front of you and you can work on it directly to make it fit.

How important is research in your working process?
You research to achieve an effect. For example, you want something that appears transparent to look less transparent, so you print something at the back to turn it into a new fabric. When you look into what has been created in the past, you'd be surprised at what has been done before. For example, ripping and cutting methods that were used for other purposes in the past have been adopted today to take on entirely new meanings.

Do you experience a 'eureka moment' when you know a design is working?
Definitely, and it's wonderful. It's hard to arrive at something simple, but a piece that is easy to put together yet amazing and enhancing is worth the labour.

Is there a routine to your design process?
It always starts with an abstract idea, which I share with someone who understands the process, and then I make an attempt at it. It could be a drape or a fold that you place against your body to see how it moves. You make a sketch of it and then make a toile. The toile is tried on a body and adjustments are made until it drapes nicely. I then give this form a function to which I add details, but it's important to remain aware and to be sensitive to where the quality of the piece lies.

What is the most enjoyable part of designing for you?
I love doing shows, dressing the models up and having a brief interaction with them as we prepare for a fashion show. The most difficult part of the process is the time it takes. I am quite an instant person, however, the process involves various contributors and their skills in order for it to be completed. Therefore, the team is important. The better the team, the more pleasurable the experience.

What materials are essential to your working methods?
A soft pencil and paper on which I sketch down whatever comes into my mind to vocalize the idea.

Is there a specific time of day when you are most creative?
In the evening when everyone's gone, or early morning when I've just woken up. It's when I'm alone that ideas go through my head.

How would you describe your design process?
You start with an idea or a shape or something abstract like an oil stain on a surface, and you cut out the shape it makes on calico and try to sew it together. It sounds a bit crazy, but it makes a garment in the end. It sounds quite simple here, but of course it's more complicated than this. The shapes are held together by seams and they wave along. Once they are on the body, they have a dynamic and they drape and you keep working on this for it to become the final garment.

What is the best environment for you to work in?
I think best when I'm moving and especially when I'm walking, as I don't need to concentrate too hard and can be sensitive to the different stimulations from the environment. Ideas can arrive during these situations.

A dress is made in toile fabric and draped on the stand for the '+5'' collection for Autumn/Winter 09/10. Adjustments and changes are made on the prototype on the stand. When the design is perfected, the garment will be constructed in the final fabric.

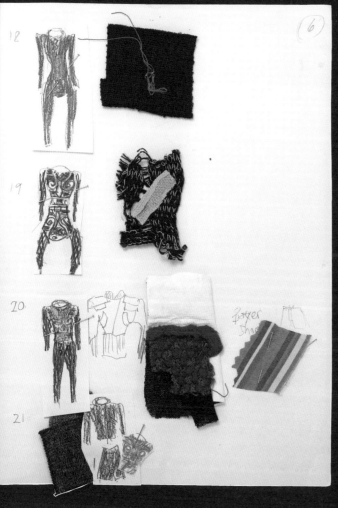

Loose design drawings with fabric swatches show how the fabric informs the design of Westwood's garments. Fabrics are layered over each other to communicate how the looks will work as a whole. All design sketches are for the '+5'' collection from Autumn/Winter 09/10.

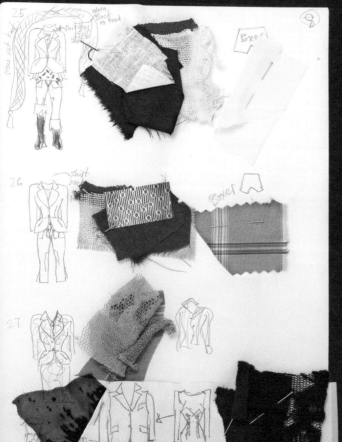

What is the most enjoyable part of designing for you?
I like all the steps, I love the time I spend on research, and I'm always really excited when I start to draw the final sketches.

WALTER VAN BEIRENDONCK

Belgian Walter Van Beirendonck graduated from Antwerp Royal Academy of Fine Arts in 1980 and presented his first collection, 'Sado', in 1983. In 1987, he showed a collection in London with five other Belgian designers, who famously became known as 'The Antwerp Six'. Van Beirendonck's clothes are known for their colourful appeal and mix humour with pop culture and science fiction with safe sex. His design slogan, 'Kiss the Future', underlines his commitment to innovation and creating groundbreaking fashion.

What fuels your design ideas?
My library, my collection of dolls, ethnic tribes and rituals and my favourite artists.

How would you describe your design process?
My design process is rather spontaneous and chaotic. In-between the other commercial collections and projects, I think all the time about what I want to do in the new WVB collection. I collect ideas in my travel sketchbook (reminders), and I start to create a total look in my head, a look from top to toe, included styling, casting and make-up. When I feel that the time is right, I sketch and colour, and put these total looks on paper. As you will see from my drawings, the final look on the catwalk is extremely close to what I sketched. I try to let my brain work and 'translate' the research to make scrapbooks with collages. I combine words and images to create an atmosphere that I like and I make a kind of mood board in the scrapbooks. At the beginning of the process, I decide the colours (everything is specially dyed for me) and make a clear colour card, and I select, make and print the fabrics.

What are your sources of inspiration?
Everything, including magazines, books, films and exhibitions. Also, I take photographs of what inspires me. I print them out, and I make small inspiration books as a reminder.

How important is research in your working process?
Research, for me, is to see and wander around, visit museums, see exhibitions, read books, surf the Net. Anything can be an inspiration. My big treasure is a huge library with hundreds of books, a lot about ethnic tribes and rituals. But each time there is 'something' that I'm attracted to and that becomes the general theme or story of the collection.

TOP LEFT — Illustrations are integral to his design process as they capture and communicate the humour, colour and energy of his collection. Shown here is an illustration for the 'Sexclown' collection from Spring/Summer 08.

TOP RIGHT — 'Kinky Kings' design from the 'Wonderland' collection for Autumn/Winter 96/97.

BOTTOM LEFT — 'Bears' concept outfit illustrated for the 'Wonderland' collection for Autumn/Winter 96/97.

BOTTOM RIGHT — The 'Gender?' collection for Spring/Summer 2000 explores a popular theme for the designer.

An illustration for the 'Cloudy Stars' collection by
Walter Van Beirendonck for Autumn/Winter 04/05.

A scrapbook page from the 'Wonderland' collection for Autumn/Winter 96/97, communicating how the designer brings together inspirational imagery. W&LT (Wild & Lethal Trash) by Walter Van Beirendonck.

A scrapbook page from the 'Welcome Little Stranger' collection for Spring/Summer 97. W&LT (Wild & Lethal Trash) by Walter Van Beirendonck. The tomato head sculpture is artwork by Paul McCarthy.

Is there a specific time of day when you are most creative?
Late at night or very early in the morning, when I reflect a lot about everything, not just creative thoughts but also about life in general.

Is there a routine to your design process?
The design process, I believe, has to be an organic one with no constraints or great methodologies behind it.

Do you have a team that is involved in the design process? If so, what do they do?
Yes, definitely. In every fashion house there needs to be a team. In my case, I do not send anything out to be sampled; everything is done in-house, from pattern making to cutting to sewing. The sampling process is very important to me, as I truly believe that it imbues the creations with a certain artisanal quality that can't be duplicated anywhere else.

What materials are essential to your working methods?
I always draw with a 6B pencil on butter paper. Over time, this paper turns yellow, giving the drawing a certain character. And I love its no-frills quality and crisp feel, it's very light and easy to manipulate.

WOODS & WOODS

Jonathan Seow studied fashion at Raffles Design Institute in Singapore, but before graduating he went to work for Singapore's only other international brand, Song & Kelly, in 1997. In 2001, Seow established Woods & Woods and has showcased his collections in Seoul, Tokyo, Paris, Berlin, Hong Kong and Australia. Woods & Woods has developed a clean and modern aesthetic that is distinct in Asia. Presenting his clothes to an international audience, Seow is at the forefront of the new wave of contemporary designers from Singapore.

Does your design process involve photography, drawing or reading?
My design process encompasses various activities, but mostly depends on a certain timeline, and the function of it. Reading, drawing and photography all form part of the process. Sometimes, I'll photograph each garment during the sampling process to help me to understand and get a better overview of what I am trying to achieve with the collection. It can also inform my next few pieces, and I design and work on garments that either complement or, from a contrary viewpoint, break the flow of the collection, all of which informs how I want the final collection to look and what it represents.

How would you describe your design process?
It is mostly personal. The process enables me to engage myself deeply with the state of things, while creating works that are a reflection of myself, society, reality versus novelty, the past and present. My main objective is to create an inner emotion for my work – work that is soulful and meaningful to me.

How important is research in your working process?
Research helps me to rationalize form and meaning. Mostly, it gives my work an authenticity, blurring the boundaries of what is mass-produced and handmade in modern times. Research helps to leave a mark on my garments beyond the runway shows and the editorial pages. It begins as an intuition, a mood follows, then fabric and form come after. My research process mostly happens during the second phase, when I am trying to find the right mood to express my current instinct. My intuition originates from my response to the current state of things. The mood and research help me to establish a voice that is stronger in pushing the idea forward.

What is the best environment for you to work in?
Usually, I either work in my studio (during working hours) or in my room at weekends. The best environment for me equates to a free state of mind. It doesn't matter where I am physically, but over breakfast on a nice morning sure helps.

How does your research and design work evolve from 2D to 3D?
The magical transformation from 2D to 3D probably takes place during the third phase of the design process, when the fabric and form come in, bringing with them all the options and possibilities of a certain shape, cut, drape and functionality versus the reality, in terms of technical barriers and other administrative issues, that is at the very core of making clothes.

What are your sources of inspiration?
I only watch a film to take my mind off designing. But a film can move me emotionally, so it naturally inspires me when I am thinking about and studying the human subject. Similarly, books form a good documentation of an ever-changing society. These are all very important in shaping my thoughts as a designer and a person.

What is the most enjoyable part of designing for you?
Research becomes meaningful when it enhances you as a person far beyond the collection. This can also mean that you learn something new, of which you may not have been totally aware before, something that is worldlier and culturally enhances your perspective on life. The challenges come when you are trying to apply your research, giving form to it by designing a garment, turning words and thoughts into a 3D object that has to function as a piece of clothing to protect a person from the weather, etc.

Designer Jonathan Seow photographs work-in-progress garments on a fitting form or mannequin to access the whole look. All looks are for the Autumn/Winter 09/10 collection. Photography Mark Lim.

Trimmed interlinings that will be used for tailored garments. Photography Mark Lim.

PAGE 195 — **BACK IMAGE** —Woods & Woods' atelier, showing garment samples and an inspiration wall and story board for the Autumn/Winter 09/10 collection. Photography Mark Lim.
FRONT IMAGE — A story wall featuring looks from the Spring/Summer 08 and Autumn/Winter 06/07 collections. Photography Mark Lim.

WOODS WOODS MAN A/W 09-10
A. B. SHIRT (COLOR-STUDIED)

WOODS WOODS MAN A/W 09-10
A. B. SHIRT (LINE-STUDIES)

WOODS & WOODS A/W 09-10
VAVARA STEPANOVA DENIM-STYLE JACKET

WOODS & WOODS A/W 09-10
MAYAKOVSKY FUTURIST POET READING JACKET

WOODS & WOODS MAN A/W 09-10
MAYAKOVSKY PARACHUTE TROUSERS

WOODS & WOODS MAN A/W 09-10
CLUB BACK UNDERWEAR SHIRT

Accurate flat line drawings are created to communicate the construction and design of each garment in the Autumn/Winter 09/10 collection. 'I definitely witness a sense of satisfaction within the team when we have found the simplest way to produce something that is complicated, and you therefore know this is the only way to go,' explains Seow.

OPPOSITE — The designer's sketchbook for the Autumn/Winter 09/10 collection entitled 'Stranger than Fiction'.

Born in Tokyo in 1943, Yohji Yamamoto studied law before attending Bunka Fashion College. He presented his first womenswear collection in the early 1970s and has developed a unique approach to clothing design.

YOHJI YAMAMOTO

Often considered as having an 'anti-fashion' approach to fashion, Yamamoto creates sculpted, asymmetrical, often oversized pieces that are layered and starkly monochromatic. His influences are varied, from traditional indigenous Japanese clothing to photographs of German rural workers in their everyday clothes, as well as uniforms and industrial workwear.

Yamamoto's original 'look' emerged from punk, but was also based on the kimono and his desire to give its shape a new energy. 'Sometimes my garments are a little difficult to wear. You need some kind of will, because my clothing is not perfectly finished, it's a little undone, so you have to wear it with spirit,' explains Yamamoto. 'I help women to move, to act, to walk, to behave naturally. My favourite connection between the body and the garment is space or air. Then, it appears that the actions or motions or silhouette are more beautiful, and I like it.'

Classical and sensual garments result from Yamamoto's ability to combine traditional Japanese garment influences, such as the kimono and the obi, with modernist ready-to-wear Western fashion. 'I want to achieve anti-fashion through fashion. That's why I'm always heading in my own direction in parallel to fashion. Because if you're not waking up what is asleep, you might as well stay on the beaten path.'

Regarded as an accomplished drawer, Yamamoto created an illustrated notebook, *Talking to Myself*, which explores his approach and that of his team. The book is punctuated with images by Nick Knight and Peter Lindbergh. By 'talking to himself' and with philosopher Kiyokazu Washida about himself and the objects he creates, Yamamoto strives to convey his attitude towards clothing.

Yamamoto's concept of 'anti-fashion' is groundbreaking. His approach to colour and shape raises new questions about what is considered beautiful in fashion, and his clothes are revered for their original and artisan style.

OPPOSITE — **TOP & BOTTOM** — The Yohji Yamamoto design team work backstage on styling the garments together before the Autumn/Winter 02/03 show. Photography Donata Wenders.
MIDDLE — Backstage during the Spring/Summer 01 show. Photography Paolo Roversi for *Talking to Myself* by Yohji Yamamoto.

Yamamoto adjusts garments on the model before the Spring/Summer 01 show. Photography Paolo Roversi for *Talking to Myself* by Yohji Yamamoto.

OPPOSITE — TOP —
Design sketches showing
ideas in progress.
MIDDLE — An exact replica
of Mrs Shimosako's office, head
of Yohji Yamamoto's ateliers in
Tokyo, April 2005. Copyright:
Gael Amzalag for Yohji
Yamamoto 'Juste des vêtements'
exhibition, at Musée de la Mode
et du Textile, Paris, 2005.
BOTTOM — The clothing
rails show toiles made between
2003 and 2005. They are all
designs in development and
some of them have never been
put into production.

Design drawings by Yamamoto demonstrate the designer's fluid
and expressive drawing that suggests the silhouettes of the garments.
Taken from *Talking to Myself* by Yohji Yamamoto, 2002.

Published in 2010 by
Laurence King Publishing Ltd
361–373 City Road
London EC1V 1LR
United Kingdom
Tel: +44 20 7841 6900
Fax: +44 20 7841 6910
email: enquiries@laurenceking.com
www.laurenceking.com

A catalogue record for this book is available from the British Library.

ISBN: 978-1-85669-683-8

Editorial Assistant: Lindsay May

Cover design — Melanie Mues, Mues Design
Cover image — Design drawing by Yohji Yamamoto, from his book *Talking to Myself*, 2002
Page 208 — Rolls of fabric stored in the Woods & Woods studio. Photography Mark Lim

Printed in China

ACKNOWLEDGMENTS

Thank you to all the brilliant fashion designers and their teams for supporting this project. The book is indebted to all the creatives that generously provided original and unpublished material, consent to document their creative processes and invaluable time for interviews. Access to drawings, sketchbooks, process work, archives, design studios and behind-the-scenes practice was a unique privilege.

Thanks to everyone at Laurence King and the team that supported the book: Helen Rochester, John Jervis, Catherine Hooper and Lewis Gill. Thanks to Lindsay May for her spreadsheet skills and super organization. A sincere appreciation to ByBoth, for brilliant art direction and for always finding the appropriate solution. Finally, thank you to everyone at Central Saint Martins, an extraordinary art school that continues to motivate and inspire me.